Fifty Hikes
in the
White Mountains

Backpackers approaching Mt. Goose Eye

Fifty Hikes in the White Mountains

Hikes and Backpacking Trips in the High Peaks Region of New Hampshire

THIRD EDITION, REVISED AND UPDATED

Daniel Doan

Photographs by Fred Bavendam

Backcountry Publications
Woodstock,
Vermont

Library of Congress Cataloging in Publication Data

Doan, Daniel, 1914—
  Fifty hikes in the White Mountains.

  Rev. ed. of Fifty hikes. Updated 2nd ed. 1977.
  1. Hiking-White Mountains (N.H. and Me.)—
Guide-books. 2. Backpacking—White Mountains
(N.H. and Me.)—Guide-books. 3. White Mountains
(N.H. and Me.)—Description and travel—Guide-books.
4. New Hampshire—Description and travel—1951-   —
Guide-books.   I. Title.
GV199.42.N42W482   1983   917.42'20443   83-2602
ISBN 0-942440-12-9 (pbk.)

Published by Backcountry Publications, Inc.
Woodstock, Vermont 05091

Printed in the United States of America

Text and cover design by Wladislaw Finne

Photographs on pages 52, 59, 93, 120, and 191 by Daniel Doan.
All other photographs by Fred Bavendam.

Third edition: second printing, updated

An Invitation to the Reader

Developments, logging, and fires all take their toll on hiking trails, often from one year to the next. If you find that conditions along these fifty hikes have changed, please let the author and publisher know, so that corrections can be made in future editions. Address all correspondence to:

Editor, *Fifty Hikes*
Backcountry Publications, Inc.
P.O. Box 175
Woodstock, VT 05091

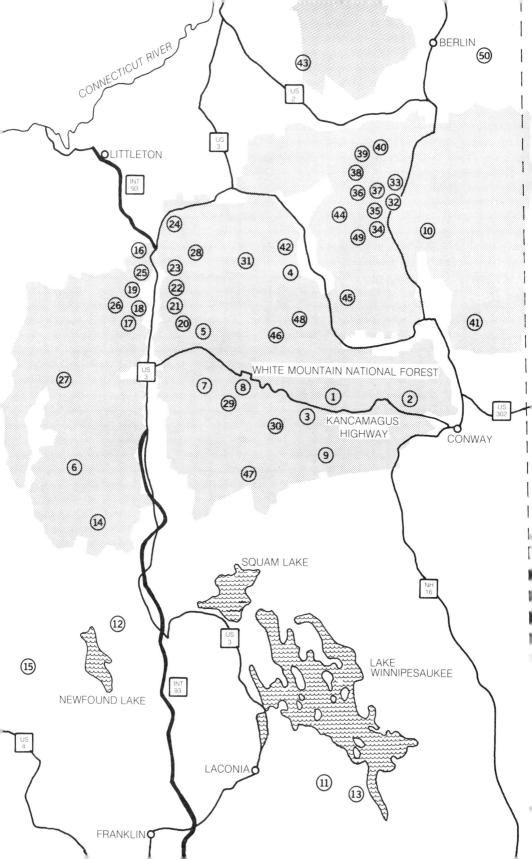

Contents

Backpacking Hikes

Introduction

These excursions into New Hampshire's White Mountains are intended to initiate the beginner and entertain the experienced hiker. There are forty-five day hikes and five overnight backpacking hikes. They are arranged from short to long and from gradual to steep. The first five hikes are suitable for family outings. Then there are five woods walks, five hikes in small mountains, and thirty hikes in and around the Franconia Range and the Presidential Range. The five backpacking hikes run from a weekend to a week. Some of the hikes loop around to their starting points, which are, of course, the places where you leave your car. Other hikes follow the same route up to their destinations and back.

Most of the hikes are within the central White Mountains. There are several that take you to lesser-known outlying summits. The corners of the hiking territory are: Mount Major (Hike 13), southeast near Lake Winnipesaukee; Mount Cardigan (Hike 15), southwest near Canaan; Mount Starr King (Hike 43), northwest in Jefferson; and Old Speck Mountain (Hike 50), northeast at Grafton Notch, Maine. Within this area, the hikes take you up all the major peaks of the White Mountains. The map facing the title page shows clearly the location of each hike.

The White Mountain hiking season extends from May into October. Winter weather occurs early and late. Above treeline, you may encounter icy storms at any time, even during the season. June and July have their black flies and mosquitoes; you'll need insect repellent. To my mind, September is the best hiking month. The heat of July, the August haze, and the bugs are gone for the season. Cool air and clear blue skies offset the customary September storms.

The Trails

The hikes follow established, well-marked trails maintained by the U.S. Forest Service, the New Hampshire Division of Parks, the Appalachian Mountain Club (AMC), and various other clubs. Forty-five of the hikes are in the White Mountain National Forest or in nearby state reservations. Some of the hikes begin on, or cross, land owned by lumber companies, by Dartmouth College, or other private property. On trails crossing boundaries between private land and the National Forest, the Forest Service posts small yellow signs at the boundaries. Any abuse of the privilege granted to hikers on this private land could result in No Trespassing signs.

The mountain trails change due to slides, washouts, new beaver ponds, trees downed by winds, and heavy use. On the other hand, some, like the Crawford Path, have hardly changed in more than a hundred years. When necessary, trails, or sections of them, are relocated. Access roads and parking places may be restricted or relocated. For latest information, check with the

U.S. Forest Service, the Appalachian Mountain Club, or the New Hampshire Department of Resources and Economic Development.

The diagrammatic maps for each hike are to provide a general outline and guide of the route. As on most maps, the top is north. For a better understanding of the trails and the mountains you should get the maps put out by the United States Geological Survey (USGS) and by the Appalachian Mountain Club (AMC). These maps show contour lines, by which you can envision the steepness of mountain trails—or lack of it. The USGS maps are being brought up to date in some quadrangles by aerial surveys and enlargement to correct the original maps and surveys of the 1920s and 1930s. But the older maps are still useful because the earth's contours haven't changed. The AMC maps are kept as modern as possible by reissues with each edition of the *AMC White Mountain Guide.* Maps may be bought at sporting goods stores and book stores, or may be ordered by mail from the Survey.

Logging Roads

The descriptions of the hikes refer often to logging roads. Almost all of these are *old* logging roads and have become part of the new forests. They are not raw bulldozed cuts for heavy modern logging machines. Only the trails keep them open. The old roads were graded for horses and sleds; although plentifully strewn with rocks, they follow the slopes at gentle angles. Together with the former railroad grades along the valleys, these old logging roads provide the best walking in the mountains.

The present logging operations supervised by the Forest Service usually leave the trails in wooded corridors. When you look off from various summits, you will see the clearcuts as irregular squares or rectangles of slash or sprouts. Many new access roads lead to these clearcuts, and such roads are often gated.

A fascinating former logging territory, and a splendid example of new forests on land once devastated by logging and fires, is the area known as the Pemigewasset "Wilderness," those mountains and valleys east of Lincoln drained by the East Branch of the Pemigewasset River. It's not really a wilderness any more; a network of trails connects with the main Wilderness Trail, which runs up the river from the Kancamagus Highway. Part of the White Mountain National Forest, the watershed includes the 18,460-acre Lincoln Woods Scenic Area. For a day hike into the Pemigewasset "Wilderness," see Hike 5; for backpacking, try Hike 48.

Distance, Walking Time, and Vertical Rise

Each hike description begins with the figures for distance, walking time, and vertical rise. These are gauges by which you can evaluate the hikes.

The times allow for leisurely climbing, which seems to me the only pleasant and sensible way, but they do not include rest periods, lunch breaks, view gazing, or bird watching. Young, hardy climbers may cut the times in half.

The vertical-rise figure tells you the approximate distance up. If you start at a 1,000-foot elevation and climb to a 2,500-foot summit, you may walk two miles or five, but your vertical rise is 1,500 feet. Sometimes you climb down into a valley and up again to a summit; your return trip will thus include some climbing, which is included in the total, or round-trip, vertical rise figure. As a

On Mt. Lafayette

general rule, you can expect that the greater the vertical rise per mile, the more strenuous the climb.

The White Mountain National Forest

The State of New Hampshire had disposed of its public land by the mid-1800s, and logging began in earnest after the Civil War. Men with axes felled trees throughout the north country—except in the White Mountains' most remote valleys, where the steep slopes presented transportation problems. The rivers were too shallow and rocky for log drives.

Because of this and other difficulties, the forests of red spruce, pine, hemlock, and cedar in the White Mountains remained standing until late in the era, and some were bypassed completely as lumbermen cut a swath from Maine to Minnesota.

Finally, railroads opened the valleys in the 1880s and 1890s, and much of the timber was cut by 1900. Logging continued through the First World War and even as late as the 1930s, but, long before the cutting was complete, forest fires had devastated large tracts of cut-over land.

Conservationists, led primarily by the Society for the Protection of New Hampshire Forests, came to the rescue of the White Mountains in the early 1900s. The federal government purchased areas for watershed protection under the Weeks Bill, beginning in 1912. By 1982, the White Mountain National Forest had grown to 752,648 acres, a portion of which extends into Maine.

The land is managed by the U.S. Forest Service under directives based on "multiple use." Among these uses are timber production, watershed protection, recreation development, and wildlife protection. Nine Scenic Areas and the Great Gulf and Presidential–Dry River

Wildernesses (both on Mount Washington) preserve a total of 54,488 acres of valleys, ponds, and mountains in their natural beauty.

Trees and Animals

The mountainsides are now covered by hardwood forests of beech, maple, yellow birch, and white birch, which took over after the destruction of the spruce. Evergreens remain predominant in the swamps. The upper summits, from about 3,000 feet to treeline, are green spruce/fir forests interspersed with white birch and mountain ash.

You will meet no dangerous animal life. This is not rattlesnake country. Black bears and wildcats are shy. I recall only six bears in fifty-five years of walking the mountains, and they were all going away fast when they became aware of me. I never saw a wildcat in the woods. Porcupines can be dangerous to an aggressive dog; otherwise they mind their own business. Even *Homo sapiens* seems gentler in the mountains.

White-tailed deer are forest denizens seldom seen in the higher mountains. You probably won't see one of the eastern coyotes now roaming the region; they survive by avoiding men, and have been doing so successfully since their arrival about ten years ago. You may see a moose. They are becoming more common, you'll certainly see their ox-like tracks. Fishers, otters, mink, and weasels are not often seen. You'll probably see a snowshoe rabbit flash quickly into cover. Red squirrels and chipmunks will chatter at you. Coons, skunks, foxes, and flying squirrels come out at night.

In the text I mention birds because I like to watch them. (Ravens are common now but were not when I described the hikes first in 1972.) Trees, flowers, and plants mean more if you know their names. Field books to identify these, the birds, and the animals, will increase your enjoyment. I also recommend Hikes 1 and 2, which follow Forest Service nature trails, as introductions to the life of the woods.

Clothing and Equipment

Careful consideration and selection of the clothing and equipment for your hikes are essential. Basic apparel includes a cotton-polyester blend shirt, walking pants or shorts, comfortable underwear, and hiking shoes worn over two pairs of socks. You should consider the modern lightweight hiking boots. They are based on designs and materials from jogging shoes. During a long hike in these boots you can avoid lifting a ton or more of the boot-weight required if you had worn a pair of the clumpers. I wear canvas and leather with a relatively thin lug sole, about two pounds—but not for backpacking. And even for hiking, if your feet aren't accustomed to mountain trails, you need the protection of a more conventional leather boot.

As long as the weather is fair, the above clothing is all you'll need to wear. Pack the rest of your equipment and spare clothes in a strong, waterproof knapsack, usually called a "day pack." Don't dangle equipment from belt or shoulder straps. No bulging pockets. Here's what you'll need: heavy wool shirt, sweater, or insulated jacket; poncho or rain suit with hood; nylon parka or shell; hat; gloves; warm pants; matches and firestarter in a waterproof container; compass; map and guidebook; pocketknife with can opener and screwdriver (Girl Scouts have a nice light one); a quart of water in a canteen or other container; lunch; and spare food for two meals.

You should consider a parka made of one of the laminated materials that are microporous, making them both breathable and waterproof. There are many such parkas in a wide range of styles and uses. The materials are also used for rain pants and the uppers of boots. Though expensive, this type of clothing can eliminate your other rain gear for active, sweat-inducing exercise, but don't expect a miracle of total sweat evaporation. Such a parka can be substituted at times for a windproof shell.

If you're backpacking, you'll need everything on the day hiker's list and more. In addition to an adequately large pack (too varied for discussion here), you'll want to take a tent, or at least a waterproof tarp; a hiker's gasoline or cartridge-type gas stove, cook kit, forks and spoons; a sleeping bag in a stuff sack; a foam pad to place under your sleeping bag at night; a small first aid kit, including moleskin for foot blisters (no snakebite kit necessary, but take insect repellent); soap and a towel; a small flashlight, two candles, and extra matches in a waterproof container; a small hatchet or saw (optional); light nylon cord for a variety of uses; and meals for each day of the trip. Food should be light and easy to prepare. Include ready-to-eat food for lunches. Standard necessities can be found at your supermarket: oatmeal, sugar, dried milk, tea, salt, hardbreads, cheese, canned meats, dried soups, etc. At your backpacking shop choose freeze-dried foods for super-light nourishment.

Equipment is no substitute for experience. Learning how to walk in the woods is more important than the best hiking boots money can buy. Break in your boots completely before you commit your feet to a long hike in them. This applies to both standard leather boots and the lightweights. If you are in a hurry to break in a pair of leather boots, put them on over two pairs of wool socks and then stand in a tub of water. Go for a walk, and walk the boots dry. They'll be broken in. Heavy mountaineering boots are unnecessary for these hikes.

As for socks, one pair of light wool socks under one pair of heavy wool socks seems to be the best combination. Pants should be loose. Fishnet undershirts are great: they keep you cool, keep you warm, pad your back under a pack, and stop insects from biting through your outer T-shirt. Down-filled jackets are comfortable beyond dreams as long as they're dry, but, when they're wet, I wish I had on that warm-though-wet product, wool.

I like a plastic transparent compass with movable base for setting a course. (Note: In the White Mountains your compass points about sixteen degrees west.) I also use plastic flask-shaped water bottles (one-pint size) instead of a canteen. Two pack easily and fit into a mountain pool to fill. I carry a small cup to fill them from trickles.

Because equipment for backpacking is so extensive, and the choice arouses such vehement contention, you may want to read a book on the subject and explore a shop or catalog that specializes in backpacking and mountaineering equipment. If you are new to backpacking, I suggest you rent your pack, tent, and other gear for the first few trips to learn what you will want to buy. What ever you finally decide to take, be sure to set everything up at home and try it out before heading into the mountains.

Rules and Regulations

All rules and guidelines for hikers in the White Mountains, both those of the Forest Service and those promoted by the Appalachian Mountain Club, have been developed to save the forest from its greatest enemy, fire, and to preserve the areas that are becoming more and more popular, especially those with delicate ecology near treeline and above in the alpine zone. The days of the roar-

ing campfire and the woodsman's bough bed are over.

The rules apply mostly to campers and backpackers, rather than to day hikers. Common sense and thoughtful consideration of others will go far to direct your behavior into conformation with rules, but there are some regulations you should know about. Hikers on private property cannot legally build wood or charcoal fires without the landowner's permission and a fire permit from the district fire chief. Use a portable stove. No overnight camping is allowed on private property without the landowner's permission. Carry out all your trash. Don't cut trees or boughs or destroy plants. Park your car well off roads. Don't park in any opening into the woods no matter how ancient, and of course never in any logging road or in front of a gate. A state law prohibits obstruction of a right-of-way.

For the White Mountain National Forest the long-standing requirement of fire permits was discontinued in 1985. There are, however, special regulations about camping and fires. You should get the latest seasonal information from the office of the Forest Supervisor in Laconia, or from district ranger stations in Conway, Gorham, Plymouth, Bethlehem, and Bethel, Maine. The Forest Service also maintains information centers located near I-93 at Campton and Lincoln and on the Kancamangus Highway at Passaconaway.

The AMC offers information at Pinkham Notch Camp, at Lafayette Place in Franconia Notch, and at the former depot near the Crawford House site.

The State of New Hampshire has rules for its Parks, Reservations, and Forests. In general no camping or wood or charcoal fires are allowed outside designated campgrounds and picnic areas. Regulations are posted. The N.H. Division of

Along the trail on Belknap Mountain

Parks and Recreation provides a brochure, "N.H. Camping Guide."

Although in the White Mountains National Forest fire permits are no longer required, you must obtain and abide by a map and rules for Restricted Use Area limitations on camping and fires. Where overuse has compacted the soil and damaged plants and trees, natural recovery is encouraged by RUAs and future harm prevented. Furthermore, no camping is allowed above treeline, which has been set at the altitude where trees are less than eight feet high. Similar restrictions—no camping, no wood or charcoal fires—are in effect on land 200 feet from many trails, and within ¼ mile around various huts, shelters, tent platforms, and lakes. (Two hundred feet is hardly enough distance to stay away from *any* trails when pitching your tent, at least to my mind.) Certain roadsides have ¼ mile RUA protection. On trails in the national forest you'll be alerted by signs posted at RUA boundaries. The back of the RUA map gives you explanations of the areas. You should also study the lists of forest ethics and safety precautions. The forest service offers helpful brochures on recreational uses of the national forest.

Camping permits are required for overnight in the Great Gulf Wilderness, June 15 through September 15. Permits and reservations are issued by the district ranger in Gorham. You need no camping permits for the Presidential–Dry River Wilderness. Day hikes in either Wilderness do not require permits.

I cannot emphasize enough your obligation to stay on trails when you are above treeline. Fragile alpine plants are at the mercy of hiking boots and once damaged may never recover. The mountains and your fellow hikers deserve an uncluttered trail. No litter, no trash left behind. And no random elimination—to put it politely, copy the cat, and make sure you're a hundred long paces away from any trail, stream, pond, or spring. No candy wrappers, no cans or aluminum envelopes or any of the slick packages our civilization provides us for throwing away. If you take them in, take them out again in your pack. The motto is: "Carry in and carry out!" And another: "Leave only your footsteps."

Huts and Shelters

In the White Mountains the Appalachian Mountain Club and the Forest Service maintain most of the trails and shelters. Open-front shelters of logs or boards face stone fireplaces. The Appalachian Mountain Club has built closed huts or lodges to serve hikers on its trail system.

Long a prime mover in this area, the AMC was founded in 1876 and had 26,000 members in 1982. It maintains 350 miles of trails, fifteen shelters, and eight mountain huts, three of them above treeline. In the huts, crews of college students provide meals and lodging for hikers during July and August; some of the huts are open from the middle of June into October. Winter accommodations (carry your own food and equipment) are available at two huts having caretakers, and at the Crawford Notch Cabins on the site of the former Crawford House. Inquire at Pinkham Notch Camp for reservations and rates. This center for AMC activities in the White Mountains on NH 16 is open year-round to accommodate skiers and hikers, and it also serves as headquarters for the system of trails, shelters, and huts.

A note on winter excursions: Snowshoes and cross-country skis can extend your season to almost twelve months. Both sports are fascinating but require learning and experience for full enjoyment and safety.

Physical Fitness

Good physical condition increases hiking pleasure. Without it, the more strenuous hikes are no pleasure at all, and there may be harm and danger.

If you wait until warm weather to get in shape, the arrangement of hikes in this book will break the news to your body that you're going to take it walking. Nobody has to be an athlete to succeed with Hike 1; Mount Washington is something else again. In preparation for the longer climbs in the high Franconias and Presidentials, I've included a few relatively easy hikes for each region. In the Franconia Region, they are numbers 16, 17, 18, and 19. In the Presidentials, they are numbers 32, 33, 34, and 35.

Stamina developed for walking and climbing provides not only pleasure but an important safety margin in the mountains. It's a form of insurance you can take out yourself.

Safety

Almost every year, the mountains claim some hiker's life. Storms are sudden and fierce above treeline. Trails over the bare rocks, marked only by cairns and signs at the junctions, disappear in the clouds and wind-driven rain, sleet, and snow. Electrical storms shoot down lightning that bounces from the rocks amid the torrential rain. Besides physical fitness, two precautions may help you survive these dangers. First, in the face of threatening weather forecasts, don't go mountain climbing, or go to some lesser peak or a woods trail. Second, in the face of gathering low clouds and wind at treeline, turn back. The woods and shelter are only a few steps behind you; ahead you will climb into increasingly thick fog and winds so strong you'll be unable to stand.

On many trails leading above treeline, a Forest Service sign will warn you of the dangers ahead. They aren't kidding, either; above treeline you're in hazardous territory. Perhaps this fact, along with the tremendous views and the thrill of being there on your own two feet, gives above-treeline hiking its excitement.

It's important to hike with a companion. (Two old friends hike best together; I've been lucky this way.) Stay together. This is a rule of every mountain clubber, ex-perienced climber, and all officials delegated to find the lost or injured lone hiker.

Carry a compass. Carry a map that you have studied so you know about the route and the trails. Be prepared to spend a night out in the woods or under a rock. This means carrying extra food, water, warm clothing, and waterproof outerwear in a knapsack.

Purity of drinking water cannot be assumed just because a stream is clear and cold and tumbling down a sylvan valley. It might contain *Giardia lamblia,* a common intestinal parasite, which causes delayed diarrhea, cramps, loss of ap-petite and weight, as well as other unpleasant symptoms. Among animals other than humans, beavers are likely to infect streams and ponds in the moun-tains. Boiling and disinfecting are stan-dard preventive measures. Portable filters for hikers may be perfected to remove the cysts from drinking water. The Forest Service offers a pamphlet "Is the Water Safe?" Personally, I take a chance on the purity of sidehill springs trickling from slopes so steep that even a careless, thoughtless human would be unlikely to climb up it and defecate within 200 feet of the water.

And last of all—but so important it might be first—before you set out tell someone where you're going, and give an alternate place for bad weather. Then go there, one or the other, and enjoy yourself. The hike is supposed to be fun. No bitching: not about the trail, the weather, or the world. Leave that attitude back with "civilization" and your other troubles.

I wish you years and years of great hikes in the White Mountains of New Hampshire.

Addresses

Appalachian Mountain Club
5 Joy Street
Boston, Massachusetts 02108
or
Pinkham Notch Camp
Gorham, New Hampshire 03581

United States Forest Service
Supervisor's Office
719 Main Street
Laconia, New Hampshire 03246

New Hampshire Department of Resources and Economic Development
Concord, New Hampshire 03301

Society for the Protection of New Hampshire Forests
54 Portsmouth Street
Concord, New Hampshire 03301

United States Geological Survey
1200 South Eads Street
Arlington, VA 22202

Introductory Hikes

1

Rail 'n River Forest Trail

Distance (around the trail): ½ mile
Walking time: depends on how much you look and learn
Map: USGS 15' Mt. Chocorua

At the White Mountain National Forest Passaconaway Historic Site on the Kancamagus Highway, 12.5 miles west of Conway, you'll find this ½-mile nature trail featuring twenty-eight stops keyed to a pamphlet available free at the trail's entrance. Don't avoid this walk because it seems to lack challenge; don't let the tourists dismay you. There is a wealth of information here for the hiker who truly wants to know the mountains.

Shortly beyond the sign directing you along the trail, you become aware of trees and their history in forests logged-off and grown again. You walk on an old railroad grade. The rails are gone and only depressions in the earth mark the ties. But, in the 1880s steam locomotives hauled flatcars loaded with millions of board feet of first-growth timber to mills in the lower valley.

Take your time and enjoy the trees. They are identified with their common and scientific names. You'll see not only familiar pine and spruce, but also larch, alder, black cherry, maple, white birch, poplar, and others. See rocks changing to soil that will support plants. Visit a swamp "garden" where you can study

White Birch

plants that thrive in wet ground and acid earth. Along the bank of the Swift River, you see stumps of alders and poplars gnawed down by beavers. Stop to look at the mountains named for the Indian chief, Passaconaway, who loved peace and, in 1627, organized seventeen tribes into a confederacy that, during his lifetime, lived compatibly with the white settlers. Learn how woods take over an abandoned field. Inspect forestry practices, conservation, and ecology preservation. All these will appear on future hikes, and you will recognize them. Knowledge of them will give a new meaning to the trails and mountains.

Rail 'n River Forest Trail is recommended for parents with youngsters who ask questions about the woods.

You can drive the Kancamagus Highway from either Lincoln or Conway. The distance to the Passaconaway Historic Site is shorter west from Conway, about 12.5 miles. From Lincoln, drive east 21.5 miles over Kancamagus Pass. The sign to watch for—"Passaconaway Historic Site"—hangs in front of a brown cottage on the north side of the highway.

The cottage was built by Austin George in 1810 on the flat land along the Swift River, known as Passaconaway

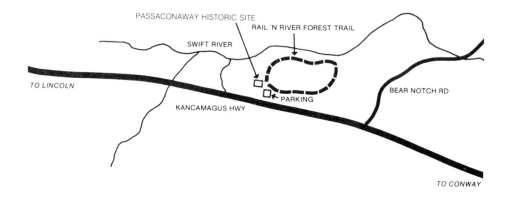

Valley or Albany Intervale. In this mountain home, beginning in 1891, Ruth Priscilla Colbath placed a lamp every night in a window, certain that her husband, Thomas, would come home. He had left the house for "a little while" that first day. He returned three years after his wife's death at the age of eighty, and found her grave in the nearby cemetery.

The restored cottage includes a Victorian country parlor and a beamed room containing mementos of the Colbaths and events of that era. In this old-time setting, you'll find modern information and Forest Service pamphlets about the White Mountains. Beside the cottage, a display room contains exhibits of stuffed animals, relics of lumbering days, maps, and posters dealing with Forest Service projects and the National Forest. Rail 'n River Forest Trail starts just east of the display room and terminates at the path behind it.

2

Boulder Loop Trail

Distance (around the loop, including spur to ledges):
 3¼ miles
Walking time: 3 hours
Vertical rise: 900 feet
Map: USGS 15′ North Conway

Hobblebush on Boulder Loop Trail

Like the Rail 'n River Forest Trail (Hike 1), the Boulder Loop Trail is for family walking and enjoyment, but it is a longer hike. Boulder Loop is keyed to stops described in the Forest Service pamphlet available at the Passaconaway Historic Site or at the Saco District Ranger Station in Conway at the corner of NH 16 and the Kancamagus Highway. At each stop you learn about glaciers, rocks, and trees. Along the trail through hardwoods and evergreens, you see examples of soil formation and forest origins from the time of the glacier fifty thousand years ago: erosion, lichens and moss, elementary plants and trees, mature specimens of oak, spruce, fir, pine, hemlock, beech, maple, birch, ash, and various other trees native to the White Mountains.

You also see boulders, a rock slide, a brook, blowdowns from a northeast storm, fracturing granite, dry slopes with plants adapted to that sunny environment, contrasting cool-moist slopes, as well as birds and flowers in season.

Descending through the magnificent hardwood forest on the return half of the loop, you'll pass on your left a clear-cut section where the mature trees have been removed for lumber and veneer, and all others cut. This is known as a silviculture system of even-aged management. You pass on into tall beeches. Watch for claw marks on the smooth gray bark. Bears climb in the fall for beech nuts.

Besides these, the trail takes you to a splendid outlook a thousand feet above the Passaconaway Valley. A spur trail leads to ledges giving views from the highest elevation. You see Mount Chocorua's sharp peak and the bulky Mount Passaconaway beyond the nearer forested ridges. These lookoffs have the built-in dangers of all cliffs.

The trail should be considered a climb rather than a picnic jaunt. Suitable shoes and other clothing are necessary. A small knapsack frees your hands of lunch, camera, and jacket. Remember to use the pack for carrying out your empty soft-drink bottles and cans and cellophane

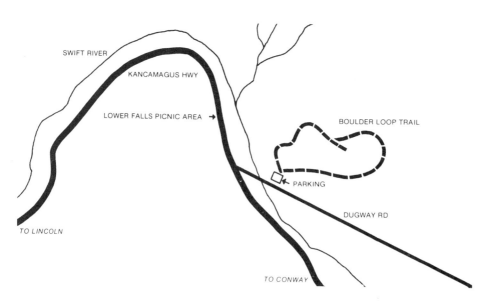

wrappers.

To reach the trail, turn off NH 16 just west of Conway onto the Kancamagus Highway. Seven miles from Conway, turn right onto the Dugway Road and cross the covered bridge over the Swift River. Watch on the left for the parking area near the Covered Bridge Campground. From the west corner of the parking area, a sign directs you to the trail, which soon forks. Bear left for the first of the information points—a rock, smoothed by the ages, extending 100 feet along the trail and reaching up 30 feet. Lichens grow on it much as they did when they were the first plants on the bare rock of the world.

3

Sabbaday Falls

Distance (picnic area to falls and back): 1 mile
Walking time: ½ hour
Vertical rise: 100 feet
Map: USGS 15' Mt. Chocorua

No more than an afternoon's jaunt, this popular short hike to Sabbaday Falls conveys an important message about the mountains. It suggests a new world to explore: one filled with outdoor sights, sounds, and sensations. It arouses a new or forgotten interest in the woods, the streams, and the miles of mountainous terrain around you.

The Sabbaday Brook Trail begins 16 miles west of Conway and NH 16 at a picnic area on the south side of the Kancamagus Highway. The graded path in a forest of maple, beech, and birch leads up to the base of the ledges through which the stream cuts its way.

A side trail, left, takes you down to the lower pool. Stone steps and peeled-log railings ease the way up the ledges above the narrow flume that was formed by water wearing away a basalt dike in surrounding granite. From a deep pothole, the stream pours down into the flume. The walkway returns to the Sabba-

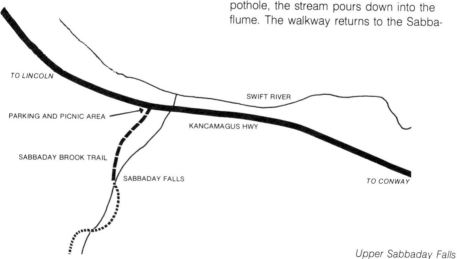

Upper Sabbaday Falls

day Brook Trail above the falls. (The Sabbaday Brook Trail continues up the brook toward Mount Tripyramid.)

Approaching from Conway, you should treat yourself to a brief stop, 12.5 miles along the Kancamagus Highway, at the Passaconaway Historic Site maintained by the Forest Service. (See Hike 1.)

Continuing west from the Historic Site, you drive past the Forest Service's Passaconaway Campground, and, after 2.5 miles you cross the bridge spanning Sabbaday Brook. Turn left for parking and the trail to Sabbaday Falls.

Westward, the Kancamagus Highway rises steadily to Kancamagus Pass at 2,855 feet, then winds down to Lincoln and I-93 at North Woodstock, about 20 miles away. Signs mark other trails into the mountains north and south. (See hikes to Black Pond, number 5; Greeley Ponds, number 9; and Mount Hancock, number 46.) Before driving the highway, check your car's gas gauge; there are no service stations on the 34 miles between Conway and Lincoln, and, across the central 15 miles, no buildings.

The adventure of driving the highway persists despite its accepted use and blacktop surface added in 1963. Before that, many tourists did not know of the completion of the gravel road's upper section, done in the summer of 1959, and uncertainty added spice. One tourist stopped near the Conway end to question an old lady rocking on her porch: "Does this road go across the mountains?" After a moment's thought she told him: "Well, a lot of cars pass by here and don't come back."

Kedron Flume

Distance (round trip): 1½ miles
Walking time: 1¼ hours
Vertical rise: 600 feet
Map: USGS 15′ Crawford Notch

Crawford Notch is a pass through the mountains. For years it provided a route between the interior Connecticut River valley and the seacoast region. Discovered by hunters in the days when New Hampshire was a royal province, and explored by settlers following the Saco River after the Revolution, Crawford Notch became a teamsters' passage be- tween sheer cliffs and steep forested slopes. The Notch is a state park now. A railroad and US 302 wind through it. But, a short distance into the woods, the mountains are still primitive and rugged.

For a brief hike into this mountain fastness, park your car at the Willey House Historical Site, 3 miles south of the Notch's gateway crags on US 302. A souvenir shop is nearby. The trail to Kedron Flume begins at a sign south of the buildings and leads from the highway up through the picnic area.

The trail is to the right of the picnic tables, which are tucked into the steep

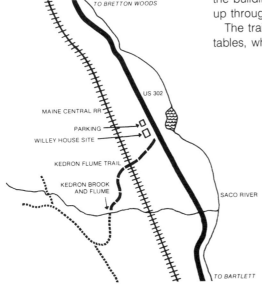

TO BRETTON WOODS

US 302

MAINE CENTRAL RR

PARKING

WILLEY HOUSE SITE

KEDRON FLUME TRAIL

KEDRON BROOK
AND FLUME

SACO RIVER

TO BARTLETT

slope. Entering the woods you soon begin climbing up twenty-four log steps. You may wish for more steps as the trail leads you to the Maine Central Railroad near the site of the earth avalanche that wiped out the Willey family in the summer of 1826. You'll find several more steps beyond the tracks.

The trail continues steep, bearing left. Although graded, with occasional log waterbars and steps, it is a mountain trail. The soft stone gravel will roll underfoot. Watch your step, especially descending. The trail leads through beech woods toward spruces farther on. It bends around a shoulder and dips into a little ravine at Kedron Brook.

The stream pours down through a narrow sluice or flume in the rock and drops over the falls below the trail's crossing. Remember rocks are slippery when wet. The outlook across the Notch's gash is to Mount Webster's southern ridge and minor cliffs.

For ½ mile past the flume, the trail twists more steeply up among big spruces and rocks to its junction with the Ethan Pond Trail, a route into the Pemigewasset "Wilderness" past the Willey Range Trail up Mount Willey, which towers above Kedron Flume.

Kedron Flume

Black Pond

Distance (round trip): 6½ miles
Walking time: 3½ hours
Vertical rise: 480 feet
Map: USGS 7½' Mt. Osceola

With only 250 feet of upgrade in the first 2½ miles, the hike to Black Pond rates as an excellent tryout for new packs and boots. The route parallels the Pemigewasset River's East Branch on an abandoned railroad bed. The sparkling water and smooth boulders are typical of mountain streams large enough to scour out a valley during the annual ice-out spring freshet.

The East Branch and its tributaries drain a territory that extends from Franconia Range's eastern slopes to the western bastions of Crawford Notch, and to Mount Carrigain and Mount Hancock on the southeast. Bounded by the Kancamagus Highway on the south, and called the Pemigewasset "Wilderness," the valley is rich in the history of men who chopped trees and earned a hard living in the forests of spruce, which they devastated. Old loggers used to look back on those days with nostalgia and tell yarns about the lumber king, J. E. ("Ave") Henry, who hired them and made a fortune. Henry, a once-barefoot poor boy, became legendary for his toughness, man driving, determination, and parsimony. The territory he clear cut, which often went up in terrible forest fires, is now largely National Forest, but the Pemigewasset "Wilderness" could tell many tales of years gone by.

The East Branch flows fast and slow. It rises and falls rapidly. Logs were successfully driven down the Pemigewasset River to Lowell, Massachusetts, in the 1850s by a state-of-Mainer, N. G. Norcross, and his red-shirted Penobscot boys, sometimes known as the Bangor Tigers. In the '90s when J. E. Henry began to cut the East Branch valley, he built driving dams to provide water flowage on which to float the logs downstream to his Lincoln mill. Many logs were too big for the river, so he built a railroad. It freed him from the temperamental water levels. The railroad grade now provides an easy path for hikers; it's known as the Wilderness Trail.

Black Pond lies in a hollow surrounded by forest, ¾ mile north of the Wilderness Trail. Covering two and one-half acres, the pond measures as much as thirty-four feet in depth, indicating the pitch of the basin it fills. Because of a boggy crossing on the Black Pond Trail as it follows the outlet brook, you might expect a shallow, marshy pond, but you'll find instead a little mountain lake in which speckled trout swim. The rocky heights to the east are the ridges of

Mount Bond. To the west is Mount Flume's pinnacle.

The Wilderness Trail, which will lead you to the branch trail for Black Pond, starts at a parking area along the Kancamagus Highway, 4.8 miles east of Lincoln. You will come to the parking area on the left just after the concrete bridge over the East Branch. Walk to the north corner toward the river and cross on the footbridge for the Wilderness Trail. Turn to the right onto its wide strip of fill. The trail follows the grade of the logging railroad, last used in 1948. There are no rails, and the ties are mostly rotted or buried, but watch out for an occasional broad-headed spike. The mixed second-growth woods are taking over after the chopping and fires. This is a popular trail

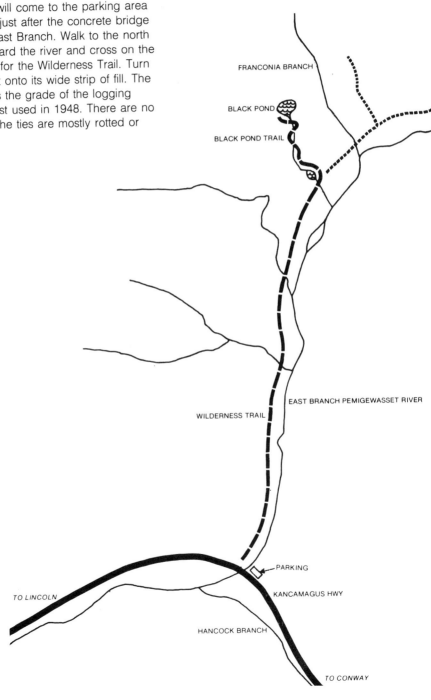

into the Pemigewasset "Wilderness," because it joins trails leading to the eastern extensions of the Franconia Range — Garfield Ridge and Zealand Ridge — and to Crawford Notch.

The Black Pond Trail branches left from the Wilderness Trail 2½ miles from the parking area and ¼ mile before Franconia Branch. For a short distance on a spur railroad grade, the trail passes a small pond, which once provided ice for the logging camps. About all that remains of the camps in the valley are rusty pieces of stoves, peavey spikes and hooks, and sled runners half-buried in the leaf mold. The occasional wild apple trees sprouted from cores thrown out the cookshack doors.

Beyond the little pond and clearing, the trail enters the woods again, ascends and descends moderately uphill between crossings of the brook for about ¾ mile to Black Pond, where it ends.

If you quietly approach the light showing ahead through the trees, you may see two deer drinking in the water. If there is a hatch of flies the trout will be dimpling the surface.

Three Ponds–Brown Brook Loop

Distance: 5½ miles
Walking time: 3 hours
Vertical rise: 500 feet
Map: USGS 7½' Mt. Kineo

A hike to Three Ponds and across a height-of-land to another watershed on Brown Brook is a leg-stretcher and fine for gaining woods experience. At a National Forest shelter near the ponds, you may cook hot dogs and beans at an open fireplace. (Carry out your trash!) A weekend in June is a good time to visit this forest environment of boggy ponds, beaver dams, hardwoods, and evergreens. Wild flowers, then abundant, will include pink lady's slipper, the little yellow flowers of clintonia, and carpets of Canada mayflower. White-throated sparrows give their haunting, north country whistles. Joining in will be all the returned birds.

But take plenty of fly dope. Blackflies will welcome you in June. Tuck long pants into socks. A head net is a wise precaution.

Drive along NH 25 west from Plymouth and turn north through Rumney to Stinson Lake. At the outlet, the road forks. Keep left along the west shore to the east end. Cross the bridge over Sucker Brook, which flows from the ponds. Drive straight past a road on the right and up the hill. Partway down the far side and .6 mile from Sucker Brook, turn left at a sign for Three Ponds Trail and parking.

You are 6.5 miles from Rumney village green.

Beyond the sign the trail leads into the woods across short logs over a trickle of water. It continues uphill among maples and birches interspersed with hemlocks and pines. Near the middle of this hill the Mount Kineo Trail leaves on the right. You will return here at the conclusion of the hike.

The trail keeps irregularly along the west slope of Black Hill and takes you past the Carr Mountain Trail on your left. About a mile farther you descend to Sucker Brook and join an old logging road, the former trail. Low ground and beaver workings in the brook indicate that you're approaching the ponds. You come to Middle Pond first. Watch for a path on the right up a steep bank. It leads to the shelter on a knoll. East of it, hidden by trees and brush, lies the smallest pond, called Lower Pond. Hardly worth visiting, its area is two and one-half acres, compared to Middle Pond's thirteen acres.

The trail continues through the woods bordering Middle Pond. Bear right near the upper end onto a bypass that avoids a boggy area. The Three Ponds Trail turns left across a washed-out beaver dam, which once formed a pond at the inlet. The Donkey Hill Cutoff continues straight past the drained pond site, now a woodsy meadow. (The Donkey Hill Cutoff—perhaps no sign—will be your route to Brown Brook and the Mount Kineo Trail leading back to the beginning hill and Three Ponds Trail near your car.)

Take the Three Ponds Trail by scrambling across the jumbled sticks of the beaver dam. Keep on through the woods ¼ mile to a spur trail on your right which leads to the Upper Pond. The Three Ponds Trail continues ahead at a red square on a tree. (It traverses forest to the Hubbard Brook Trail and NH 118, about four miles away.)

Follow the spur trail, right, a hundred yards to Upper Pond. The twelve acres

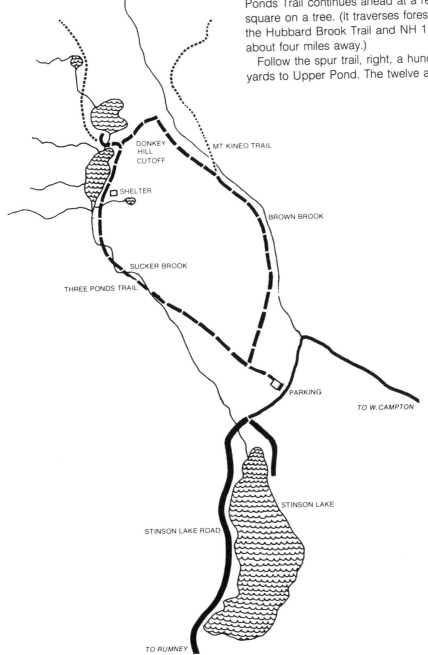

DONKEY HILL CUTOFF

MT KINEO TRAIL

SHELTER

BROWN BROOK

SUCKER BROOK

THREE PONDS TRAIL

PARKING

TO W. CAMPTON

STINSON LAKE

STINSON LAKE ROAD

TO RUMNEY

Near Three Ponds

of water at its deepest is ten feet, or four feet less than the fourteen feet for Middle Pond, but it floods into coves and boggy growths of waterbrush and evergreens. A gentle slope of woods on the south grows luxuriant wild flowers around old campsites of trout fishermen. Perhaps there'll be a swimming black duck suddenly beating aloft from the water, possibly a mink or beaver if you wait silently on shore and listen to the thrushes. After a heavy rain, you hear the falls splashing down the west ridge into the pond from tiny Foxglove Pond.

Return to the old beaver dam and junction with Donkey Hill Cutoff. Turn left. The Donkey Hill Cutoff is rather obscure as it bears right through the grassy upper end of the drained beaver slough. Then it swings sharp left to take the route of an old logging road. Climbing slightly but steadily, you cross the imperceptible height-of-land and descend more abruptly toward the bogs and beaver flowages of Brown Brook. Avoiding this wet tangle, after a view toward Mount Kineo, the trail climbs a small ridge and turns sharply right, south. You follow up and down several ridges and valleys and past a spring on your right, then swing west around a spruce swamp to the junction with the Mount Kineo Trail. Here at

ledges over which Brown Brook flows and tumbles down into lower hardwoods from the spruces, the Mount Kineo Trail crosses to the far bank. (The Mount Kineo Trail heads northward over a shoulder of Mount Kineo three and one-half miles to a Forest Service road in the Hubbard Brook Experimental Forest.)

Keep straight down Brown Brook on the Mount Kineo Trail. Had you been dropped blindfolded from a helicopter along it, you'd easily mistake it for the logging road you followed near Middle Pond. It follows the west bank of the brook for about a mile, then bears away to the right as a woods trail. (Avoid the logging road, the former trail, which continues across the brook to the road east of your car.) Watch for yellow blazes on trees.

This section of the Mount Kineo Trail leaves the valley of Brown Brook, climbing slightly across a ridge to the junction with the Three Ponds Trail. Turn left for the short walk down to your car.

The road from Stinson Lake continues east through Ellsworth to NH 3 at West Campton. Not maintained entirely in winter, it is plowed past the Three Ponds Trail. Maybe you'll be considering this loop hike for a winter ski tour.

7

East Pond

Distance (Tripoli Road to East Pond and back): 3 miles
Walking time: 2½ hours
Vertical rise: 780 feet
Maps: USGS 15′ Plymouth; USGS 7½′ Mt. Osceola

It its simple wooded setting, with Scar Ridge and Mount Osceola's West Peak in the background, East Pond resembles many small, high lakes, which nestle among the ridges and mountains surrounding the more impressive and famous peaks. Yet each is individual, a special goal for a hike. East Pond covers six and one-half acres. Much of the shore is lined with rocks, or gravel and sand. Dead trees standing in places testify to the flooding caused by beavers who build their dams at the outlet and inlet. The water is cool and clear; it reaches depths of as much as twenty-seven feet and provides shelter for speckled trout, which seem inclined to stay there.

Across Scar Ridge's spruce-grown slopes, green lines indicate the routes of old logging roads. Scrap iron and bolts lie in the sand near the pond's outlet, relics of dredging for diatomaceous earth years ago. A ditch guides the little brook to its drop-off into the valley. In late September, berries of several mountain ash trees cluster in scarlet splashes above the shore and against the ridge, making a Christmas-like display of green and red. In the spring, snow lingers in protected hollows. Hikers on Memorial Day may still find a melting drift near the outlet.

The East Pond Trail crosses Scar Ridge and five miles of woods between the Tripoli Road and the Kancamagus Highway. The shortest route to the pond is from the Tripoli Road, which leads east off I-93 at Exit 31. The Tripoli Road is better known as the access to the Russell Pond Campground. It connects with the upper end of Waterville Valley and NH 49.

Drive past the campground's entrance road on your left. About 5 miles from NH 175, watch on the left for the Forest Service signpost marking the start of the East Pond Trail. Park off the Tripoli Road. The trail begins as a gated Forest Service road to a clearcut half a mile up the ridge. As the road bears right into that opening, keep straight on the old trail. After a few yards you come to the Little East Pond Trail on the left, and you cross the railroad grade that once supported rails and trains servicing the Tripoli Mill to your right. Foundations still exist in the woods that grow from the site where the diatomaceous earth was processed.

Continue straight ahead as the trail rises gradually through hardwoods. Beyond a bridge over the outlet brook you begin to climb more steeply for the

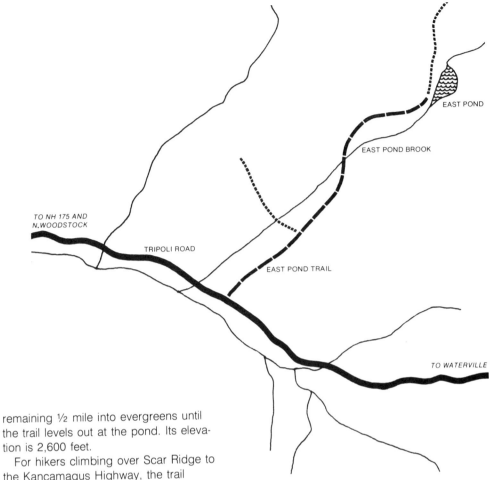

TO NH 175 AND
N.WOODSTOCK

TRIPOLI ROAD

EAST POND

EAST POND BROOK

EAST POND TRAIL

TO WATERVILLE

remaining ½ mile into evergreens until
the trail levels out at the pond. Its elevation is 2,600 feet.

For hikers climbing over Scar Ridge to
the Kancamagus Highway, the trail
passes the south end of the pond and
runs part way along the west shore
before it swings away steeply and heads
northeast for the height-of-land about 500
feet above the pond. Of course, a hiker
crossing between the two roads must ar-
range transportation at the end of his
hike.

Greeley Ponds

Distance (round trip): 4 miles
Walking time: 2½ hours
Vertical rise: 400 feet
Map: USGS 7½' Mt. Osceola

The west shoulder of Mount Kancamagus and Mount Osceola's precipitous East Peak frame the two Greeley Ponds in a wild and mountainous setting. The northern or upper pond below Mad River Notch reflects the western cliffs; the lower pond narrows between boggy shores grown to spruce and fir.

As an official National Forest Scenic Area, 810 acres surrounding Greeley Ponds are preserved in their natural beauty. To this end, the Forest Service has taken down the old log shelter by the upper pond, because, paradoxically, it was too popular. Sanitation problems, fuel requirements for the fireplace, garbage and rubbish disposal, and campsites extemporized nearby all despoiled the scanty earth, the pure water, and the slow-growing trees. People were overwhelming the delicate environment they had come to enjoy. So the Forest Service has asked overnighters to plan their trips elsewhere. Visit, but don't camp.

To reach the trail from Lincoln drive the Kancamagus Highway past the start of the Wilderness Trail (4.8 miles from Lincoln) and east of the concrete bridge above the Pemigewasset's East Branch. Follow the highway up Hancock Branch past Otter Rocks Rest Area. Drive past

the Forest Service's trail sign for East Pond on your right. About 1 mile farther (9.5 miles from Lincoln), watch for a similar brown board on which engraved lettering directs you to Greeley Ponds from a parking area.

Beyond a small knoll the trail leads over split-log and plank walkways and bridges across wet seepages and over the South Fork of Hancock Branch. Then you climb easily to Mad River Notch, which is the height-of-land above the ponds. The trail drops a short distance to the upper pond and follows under the cliffs along the west shore to a junction with the Mount Osceola Trail on the right. A spur trail, left, leads around the end of the pond to the former shelter site.

Straight ahead, the Greeley Ponds Trail continues past a spring on the right. In ½ mile it reaches the lower pond. (For almost three miles it leads west through evergreen and deciduous woods, following the young Mad River, to Waterville Valley at so-called Depot Camp, now a clearing where the Forest Service Livermore Road begins.)

The upper pond has an area of one and one-quarter acres and a maximum depth of twenty-seven feet. The lower pond averages three feet deep over its

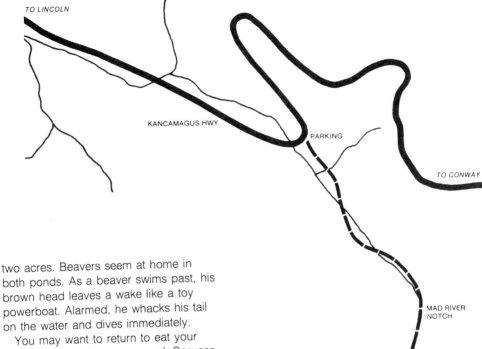

TO LINCOLN

KANCAMAGUS HWY

PARKING

TO CONWAY

MAD RIVER
NOTCH

UPPER GREELEY
POND

LOWER
GREELEY
POND

two acres. Beavers seem at home in both ponds. As a beaver swims past, his brown head leaves a wake like a toy powerboat. Alarmed, he whacks his tail on the water and dives immediately.

You may want to return to eat your sandwiches by the upper pond. Spruces and pointed firs rise toward the cliff and reflect in the still water. Speckled trout break the surface to suck down hatching flies. Juncos and white-throated sparrows call from the trees. Cedar waxwings flutter over the pond to catch bugs, then return to a tree branch alongshore and preen their glossy feathers. Swallows skim above the spruces or dip into the pond for an instant of a skimming arc after insects. Dragonflies patrol the airways.

For a bird's-eye view, climb up the steep Mount Osceola Trail as far as the ledges, about ½ mile. First, through the open spruce forest, you may notice a little-known profile to the southwest. From the rock face, the wide view centers at the tiny lake far below. Watch your step on the ledges. They are dangerous when wet or icy, and you'll want to return safely to the pond for final minutes close to an intrinsically wild harmony of water, rocks,

and trees—before you return to your car by the same route you followed up.

A Note on Overuse

The increasing popularity of the mountains creates a problem faced by the Forest Service, by the Appalachian Mountain Club, by other mountain clubs, and, in fact, by all conservationists and all citizens: overuse.

Greeley Pond

Hikers, like all mankind, congregate, and so destroy the primitive environment they seek. On Mount Washington, Tuckerman Ravine camping had to be restricted to protect the trees, plants, and soil; they are responding. In the Franconia Range, Liberty Spring Shelter has been replaced by tent platforms. Campfire and camping regulations throughout the White Mountain National Forest are being extended to preserve both the forests and the areas above treeline. The problem became so serious that the Forest Service established Restricted Use Areas (RUA) to allow natural recovery of damaged land, trees, plants, and water. Soil erosion, vegetation loss, water pollution, compaction of soil, usually at campsites, are examples of environmental damage that hikers can cause. Excessive use of campfires and the accompanying destruction of the wood resource are in need of control also. Obviously, dispersal of hikers is necessary, and an important aim of the program.

The RUA are designated by signs along the trails and roads. An excellent, color-coded map showing them is a necessary part of your hiking equipment. Explanations are on the back. Get one at the same time and place you get your fire permit. (See Introduction.)

Easy access to the mountains is certainly not the whole problem, but it may be part of it. The Kancamagus Highway accounts in some measure for the popularity of Greeley Ponds and the consequent overuse, classification as RUA, and removal of the shelter. Camping and fires are prohibited year-round at Greeley Ponds and within a ¼ mile strip on either side of the trail from the Kancamagus Highway.

Although Greeley Ponds had long been designated a Scenic Area to preserve its special beauty, this was not enough. The area is recovering, and I like to think that hikers are learning to be more careful of the forest and mountains. I am encouraged by the improvement in the litter along trails and at campsites. Hikers are responding to the motto "Carry In, Carry Out." They are also taking to heart more and more (I believe and hope) the ethics of good camping and hiking practices. You can do the same by following the list on the back of your RUA map. The RUA restrictions are in effect, with exceptions such as Greeley Ponds, from May 1 to November 1. AND most of the White Mountain National Forest has NO restrictions.

With care and preservation, the mountains can be a continuing source of "wildness" in the deepest sense, of life force from the trees, moss, lichens, birds, and animals—but only if men control their own "wildness."

Old Mast Road and Kelley Trail

Distance (round trip): 5 miles
Walking time: 3¼ hours
Vertical rise: 1,000 feet
Map: USGS 15' Mt. Chocorua

The loop from Wonalancet over the Old Mast Road and Kelley Trail connects with other trails between NH 113A and the Kancamagus Highway. The area offers hikes and climbs of varied distances and destinations in the Sandwich Range—mountains that extend west from Mount Chocorua and include Mount Paugus, Mount Passaconaway, Sandwich Mountain, and others north of the Lakes Region.

A hike need not be a physical challenge. Woods walking provides the satisfactions of escape and seclusion as well as the pleasures of striding and breathing deeply. For these purposes, the Old Mast Road—Kelley Trail combination is ideal.

According to legend, the Old Mast Road was first cut through the primeval forest to haul out great masts for the British navy. The trail's ascent up even contours toward Paugus Pass, and the long stretches without a turn, would seem to bear out the legend. For contrast, the return route takes you scrambling down Cold Brook via the Kelley Trail.

Drive to Wonalancet on NH 113A from Sandwich or Tamworth. Turn north at the corner in the meadow. Pass the post of-

fice on your left and drive a scant half-mile to a road on the right. Take it across the field to parking at a bulletin board.

Walk along the road from the parking area to the woods. At a fork and two gates closing the way to unauthorized vehicles, turn left onto the Old Mast Road. (Kelley Trail follows the right fork, which will be your return route.)

The Old Mast Road soon takes you to a bridge over a brook. (The Wonalancet Range Trail starts up on your left for those wooded summits and the Walden Trail.) Cross the bridge and walk into a clearing once used for yarding logs. Bear left and watch for a sign. The Old Mast Road becomes an unused logging road up a steady grade.

You climb through a forest of beech and yellow birch. The rugged, older, yellow birches have a reddish-brown-gray bark, scaly and furrowed, as though a different species from the younger trees with their pale yellow bark that peels across the trunks in ribbons and layers. Their leaves resemble those of the white birches sometimes growing near.

Easily distinguished are the smooth, gray, beech trunks common along the trail, which they shade by extending their muscular branches almost horizontally.

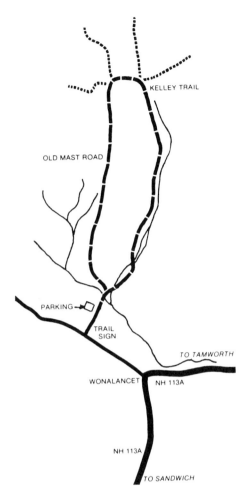

During a warm damp August, many mushroom varieties appear almost overnight. There are both edible and inedible varieties, and, of course, some very poisonous ones. Among the toxic varieties are the deadly amanita, both the yellow type and the white species known as the Destroying Angel. Fragrant orange chanterelle, smelling of apricots when warmed in your hand, shaped like a little inverted twisted saucer on a stem, is a gourmet's delight. But, unless you are an expert on the various species, don't take chances by eating any of them.

Birds along the trail are typical of the deep woods, such as thrushes, although a scarlet tanager sometimes flits and calls among the high branches, or a fluttering redstart flashes among smaller trees.

After 2½ miles, the Old Mast Road terminates at a junction on the height of land named Paugus Pass. Continuing north, descending, rough, is the Square Ledge Trail. Left, or west, the Walden Trail leads up Mount Passaconaway. Right, or east, the Lawrence Trail crosses the pass and climbs Mount Paugus. The Lawrence Trail also leads to the Kelley Trail, which is your return route for this hike.

Turn right (east) on the Lawrence Trail and follow it ½ mile to the Kelley Trail. At their junction, the Lawrence Trail continues its rough and steep ascent east up Mount Paugus. To the left (north) the Oliverian Brook Trail leads, after about four and one-half miles through wet ground along Oliverian Brook, to the Kancamagus Highway. For your return to Wonalancet, turn right (south) and follow the Kelley Trail into the ravine of Cold Brook.

Here the trail descends over rocks and past falls and through gloomy, cool woods of big spruces. A ledge split again and again looks like the stone work of an expert mason. There may be deer tracks on the miniature sand bars,

The branches end in slender twigs and light green leaves; the delicacy seems to belie their strength. The burrs enclosing the triangular nuts begin to open in late August, to the delight of squirrels and bluejays. Bears also feast on the beechnuts by climbing into the branches. Keep looking at the gray trunks and you'll see the healed gouges of claw marks—but probably no fresh ones.

After ½ hour from the parking area you come to a Forest Service road. Cross the road and continue up the Old Mast Road.

Along the Old Mast Road

maybe a winter wren on a mossy log, trilling like a coloratura canary. Lush woodland ferns grow from dark humus and curve over rocks. Hobblebush blossoms are white in early summer— they turn to green berries later, then red. Graceful, gray-green lichens thrive on ledges.

Lower down in the valley, the Kelley Trail stays on the west bank high above the brook, then descends steeply and crosses to the east bank. As you approach the last section of the trail, it crosses the same logging road that you met on the Old Mast Road, but farther east. Crunch over the gravel and enter the woods again. In 4 minutes you'll emerge on the logging road once more; it has curved 90° out of sight from the trail's brief wooded crossover. Follow the logging road out about ¼ mile to the gate and the parking area.

10

Wildcat River–Bog Brook Loop

Distance (around the loop): 6½ miles
Walking time: 4 hours
Vertical rise: 700 feet
Map: USGS 15' North Conway

This largely streamside hike is one of the most pleasant in the mountains. The Wildcat River—here a brook sparkling in the morning light—and its tributaries introduce you to a day of woodsy contrasts. From a junction in the upper Wildcat River Trail, before it heads up to Carter Notch, you turn eastward along a nearly level mile on the Wild River Trail. Then the Bog Brook Trail returns you to the Wildcat River and your car parked near the end of the Carter Notch Road, five miles north of Jackson. You may expect wet feet along Bog Brook early in the season, yet be dryshod by mid-summer.

To reach the village of Jackson driving north toward Pinkham Notch, turn off NH 16 onto NH 16A over the much-photographed covered bridge. Passing the village stores, keep left across a stone bridge spanning the Wildcat River, and at once turn to your right onto NH 16B. You pass an old hotel on the left and drive up a steep hill beside the cascades of the river on your right. Then the valley opens up toward Carter Dome, Carter Notch, and Mount Wildcat. Two miles from the stone bridge NH 16B branches to the right across a bridge. Continue straight ahead on the Carter Notch Road. It ends long before the notch, as you may suspect when it goes toward the upper valley's steep ridge, when the asphalt changes to gravel, and when you come to a log cabin back on the slope to the left. The road beyond this has been graded but may be rutted and potholed by logging trucks.

From the end of the asphalt, drive slowly for .7 mile to a fork. The right fork is the trailhead for your route, the Wildcat River and Bog Brook Trails, which coincide for about ¾ mile. There may be no signs. The right fork can sometimes be driven in dry weather for another .3 mile past a cottage on the left to a turnaround. This woods road is not for cars as low as mine. At the fork there is parking for three cars, or you may park on wide shoulders back down the Carter Notch Road.

Walk to the turnaround. At the right or southeast arc of the rough circle you'll find a sign by the Forest Service for Bog Brook Trail and one by AMC for Wildcat River Trail. You may wonder about the trail tags on trees, blue #5. They mark a ski trail route of the Jackson Ski Touring Club.

Beyond the signs the trail enters the woods at a slightly descending curve.

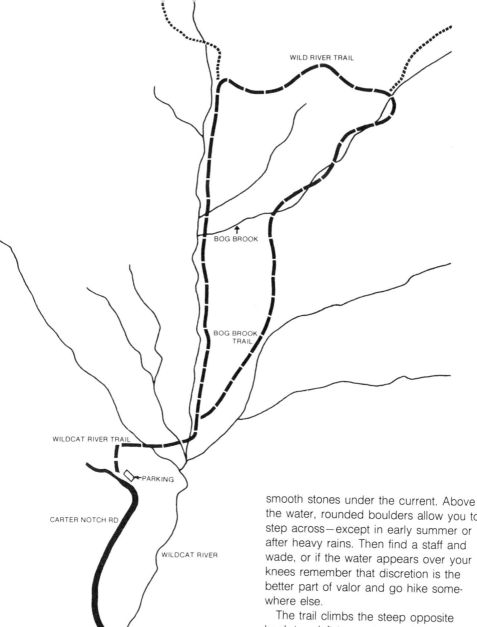

WILD RIVER TRAIL

BOG BROOK

BOG BROOK
TRAIL

WILDCAT RIVER TRAIL

PARKING

CARTER NOTCH RD

WILDCAT RIVER

TO JACKSON

You cross a tributary to the Wildcat River and soon another. A half mile from the turnaround you come to the main stream. It's so clear that the sun glints on the smooth stones under the current. Above the water, rounded boulders allow you to step across—except in early summer or after heavy rains. Then find a staff and wade, or if the water appears over your knees remember that discretion is the better part of valor and go hike somewhere else.

The trail climbs the steep opposite bank to a left turn onto an old logging road grown to grass and bushes. This shortly brings you to a sign for the Bog Brook Trail to the right. Another sign keeps you going upstream on the Wildcat River Trail. The ski touring tags are yellow #43. Trail blazes are blue paint on trees.

Ten minutes from this junction you

come to a Forest Service gravel road. On your left is a bridge over the Wildcat River. Keep straight across the road and up a bank where the trail continues along the grade you've been following.

About an hour from your car you come to Bog Brook. It falls into Wildcat River where a ledge forms a chute for its last splash. A very long step takes you across to a narrow embankment grown to alders. After a few yards the trail resumes the steady but gradual rise in open woods.

This walk is most spectacular around Memorial Day weekend when acres of trout lilies bloom yellow above their mottled leaves, overspread by birches and beeches. Along some sections of the trail, hobblebushes hold up their flat, white clusters of flowers, which can be seen for long distances through the aisles of the forest.

After you've been walking for about two hours, the first section of the hike's triangular loop meets the second section, the Wild River Trail, which now joins from the right. (The Wildcat River Trail continues to Carter Notch and the AMC hut one and three-quarters miles farther and 1,000 feet higher.) Here you should turn right up a short easy climb and then loaf along this Wild River Trail. It conforms to the contours at approximately 2,340 feet. You started at 1,700. Follow the faint impression of an old sled road. Avoid damp places by picking your way, now and then, carefully through the bushes.

Forty minutes from the Wildcat River Trail you surmount a gentle slope and look into the valley of a tributary to Bog Brook. Soon down there, you find that two long steps, one on a rock midway across the brook, take you to the opposite bank. The trail gradually curves left into spruce and balsam woods.

They extend to the junction with Bog Brook Trail on your right. You have also arrived at the boundary between Carroll County to the south, where you've been walking, and Coos County to the north. This junction is also the high point of the hike, although in the spruce woods you may not be impressed with the 2,400 feet. (The Wild River Trail continues east to Wild River Campground eight miles from the Bog Brook Trail. See my *Fifty More Hikes in New Hampshire*, Hike 50.)

Turn to the right onto Bog Brook Trail. In a few yards you are at the crossing of the brook. It's not wide—usually a long step across the break in the old dam. No more sloshing through, because the beavers are gone. In the late 1940s and for fifteen years thereafter, beavers lived in a dozen ponds along Bog Brook, and built their lodges in many of them where their dams held back water deep enough to cover the underwater lodge entrances and the winter's food of branches sunk nearby. The beavers are gone now and the local trout with them to a large extent. Whatever the cause of their disappearance from Bog Brook, their ponds no longer serve us as trout hatcheries and flood-control impoundments.

The Bog Brook Trail winds southwest to other swampy crossings and past the sites of former ponds now hidden in bushes. Then the stream tumbles down from the bog country as the trail crosses it twice more. Soon you will see the last of it as it heads for the Wildcat River. You stay to the south of it through open woods and at a swinging walk along an old logging road. You'll be reminded of the upper brook at one section of alders and muddy ground, which you can bypass to the left. Then step out again to the junction with the Wildcat River Trail.

Turn left, retracing your earlier route to the turnaround and along the road to your parked car.

I think you'll retain vivid memories of this remote little corner of the White Mountains.

11

Belknap Mountain

Distance (round trip): 1½ miles
Walking time: 1¼ hours
Vertical rise: 740 feet
Map: USGS 15′ Winnipesaukee

Lake Winnipesaukee from Belknap

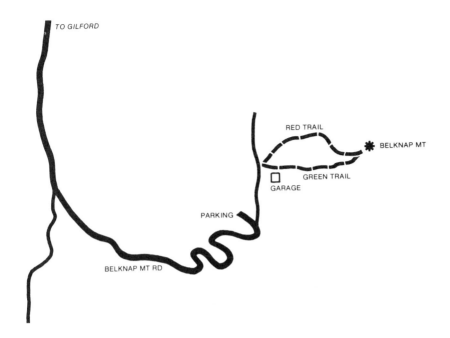

TO GILFORD

RED TRAIL

BELKNAP MT

GREEN TRAIL

GARAGE

PARKING

BELKNAP MT RD

A short climb to the lookout tower atop Belknap Mountain opens a view across Lake Winnipesaukee's blue water and many islands. The Ossipee Mountains rise beyond in impressive array, green ridge upon green ridge forming a long single mountain from this distance. To the left, fifty miles away and unmistakable in spring and fall when it alone displays snow, Mount Washington appears distant yet splendid. Nearer and somewhat in line, peaks of the central and west Sandwich Range group themselves beyond the far end of Lake Winnipesaukee. Still more to the left and again distant, the line of rocky Franconia Range is dominated by Mount Lafayette. Foothills around Mount Moosilauke fill in the panorama continuing west. On a sunny day the passing high clouds shift light and shadows upon the lake and mountains.

Of the four summits in this small, circular range south of Lake Winnipe-saukee, Belknap Mountain is the highest, although perhaps not so well known as Mount Gunstock with its ski area of the same name. Mount Gunstock and Mount Rowe are usually climbed by trails from this ski area, where information is available. The fourth summit, Piper Mountain, is a bare ridge to the south. Belknap Mountain offers not only the highest summit, 2,384 feet, but also a mountain drive to a picnic area.

Turn off NH 11A at Gilford and proceed south through the village. The road, in a residential area, makes a sharp left turn and climbs to the top of a ridge; it then turns right, and continues south under the mountain slopes to the Belknap Mountain Road, which forks left about 2 miles from Gilford. This blacktop road leads into a steep valley, winds upward, changes to gravel, resorts to switchbacks, and ends at a level parking area.

For the trails to the summit, walk uphill

along the continuation of the road and past a small garage. A wide service route on the right goes up near the telephone and TV cable lines. This is the Green Trail marked with green paint blazes. More pleasing to hikers is the Red Trail beginning on the right a few yards along a woods road. The path enters the woods and is identified by red paint blazes. It rises steadily and becomes more of a mountain trail as it bears right into spruces. It climbs left again to a junction with the Green Trail. Above, through the spruces, you see the fire lookout's woodshed and cabin. The summit is directly beyond, surrounded by spruces; ledges support the steel tower.

Belknap Mountain is worthwhile climb- ing even on a hazy day. Although distant mountains are obscured, the nearer Lakes Region and Lake Winnipesaukee's varied shorelines appear in a bird's-eye view. The lake is busy with boats. There is activity and traffic on roads in the Laconia–Weirs Beach area. For contrast, the woods stretch away east to the bare summit of Mount Major. A pond at the east base along NH 11A shows that beavers have taken over an old hay field. Belknap Mountain's blueberries resemble packaged varieties in supermarkets, but a handful will remind you what blueberries are supposed to taste like.

Return to the parking area easily by the service route, the Green Trail.

12

Plymouth Mountain

Distance (round trip): 3 miles
Walking time: 2 hours
Vertical rise: 770 feet
Maps: USGS 15' Cardigan; USGS 15' Holderness

Like Stinson Mountain to the northwest, Plymouth Mountain's high ridge is especially suitable in the spring as an introduction to a season of climbing. Or you may want to visit it in the fall when the foliage is most colorful and when snow has already chilled the more northern peaks.

Plymouth Mountain, although visible from I-93 southwest of Plymouth, is little known and unspoiled. It is steep, yet undemanding. Because it rises in the Pemigewasset River valley and has a variety of trees and terrain, the slopes are alive in May with migrating birds. Sometimes the annual arrival of the warblers happens before the leaves unfold. Then you can spot the little birds clearly. The summit's evergreens and ledges attract juncos and white-throated sparrows. You see more birds than views because the ledges at the summit are surrounded by evergreens, which grow a little taller every year, but you gain a perspective up the beautiful valley leading to Franconia Notch.

Among the many birds, the black-throated, blue warblers seem to favor Plymouth Mountain as late as the last ten days of May after the leaves are fully out. Watch for the slate-blue back of the male, with the identifying touch of white on the wings, and the black throat above a white breast. His notes are an odd buzzing series with a rising inflection at the end. Trace the sound high up in the oaks and beeches, and you may catch the singer in your binoculars.

During this latter part of May, there will be little green carpets of dwarf ginseng, the leaflets topped with frilly white blooms. The occasional large oaks, beeches, and yellow birches have an undergrowth of lesser trees sheltering other wildflowers and ferns. This forest changes to spruce and fir along the ridge in a manner typical of these New Hampshire elevations, here reaching 2,187 feet.

Follow NH 25 west from Plymouth. Turn south on NH 3A at the rotary, and drive toward Newfound Lake. Approaching the northern end of the lake, watch for the right turn to Hebron and Groton, but don't take it. Opposite this, left, is a dirt road known as Pike Hill Road. Don't attempt to drive it in the springtime or after heavy rain; instead, walk the country mile uphill to the start of the Plymouth Mountain Trail.

As the slope levels beyond a driveway on the left in the brush-grown old farm-

Indian Pipe

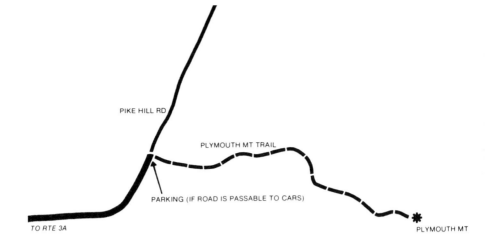

PIKE HILL RD

PLYMOUTH MT TRAIL

PARKING (IF ROAD IS PASSABLE TO CARS)

TO RTE 3A

PLYMOUTH MT

land, watch for the trail on the right-hand side of Pike Hill Road. There may be a sign on a tree. An opening through the trees is a former logging road, which leads you over a low knoll to a meadow and the remains of a beaver dam. Bear left across the trickling brook. The trail enters the woods beyond the meadow. At once you begin to climb. Markers for the trail are tin can tops nailed to trees, and small board signs, each with a stenciled black wolf in one corner, put up by Camp Mowglis.

After a steady rise, the trail swings left, gets steeper, and comes out on a bare ledge, fine for picnics. Beyond this ledge, the trail leads down and up again through spruces, mostly along the ridge, to the cairn and tree-grown rocks of the summit.

13

Mount Major

Distance (round trip): 2½ miles
Walking time: 1¾ hours
Vertical rise: 1,000 feet
Map: USGS 15′ Winnipesaukee

Steep, wooded slopes and ledges hide this bare summit above Lake Winnipesaukee's Alton Bay. Mount Major surprises you with the extent of the outlook in all directions, but you are primarily attracted to the lake, for this is a lakeshore mountain.

The scenic highway section of NH 11 runs above the west shore of Alton Bay. Five miles north from the summer resort of that name, a western ridge conceals Mount Major's flat crown. A highway sign identifies the parking area for hikers. This is .5 mile north of the parking for motorists' views across the lake. The Mount Major Trail starts from the northwest corner of the parking area, beyond the line of guard rocks, on the edge of the woods.

The trail, actually a logging road, enters a little valley of oaks, maples, and hemlocks. Almost at once it forks. Trail signs point to the right, but the left fork rejoins at the top of the slope and displays an interesting gully eroded in rotten rock. The right fork rises steeply. Rain and runoff have exposed glacial stones. After about a five-minute climb, keep to the left where a short bypass loops to the right and back to the main road.

Soon you follow a westering curve at the junction with the left fork. The road levels and is deeply rutted by logging trucks along the north shoulder of the mountain. Check your watch because your turn upward toward the summit is only ten minutes away. Old stone walls parallel the road or strike off among the oaks.

You may notice a trail to the left uphill and obviously little used. Stay on the logging road straight ahead, but watch for a branch road on your left. You could easily walk by it on the logging road. It's marked by a sign on a tree and blue blazes. This leads you upward over cobblestones away from the main, level logging road. A short climb brings you to the true mountain footpath.

It swings to the right and then to the left, winding over bare rock and among pines. It grows steeper. Approaching the first open ledges, several bypasses can be followed as they all return to the trail blazed in blue on the open rock. In early June, there are pink lady's slippers flowering. Columbine blossoms beside the rocks. As you climb the ledges, pause to look behind you for the first view of Lake Winnipesaukee.

Low-bush blueberries grow along the

Stone Hut on Mt. Major

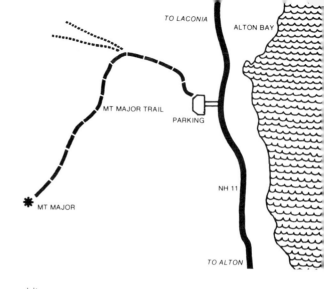

TO LACONIA

ALTON BAY

MT MAJOR TRAIL

PARKING

NH 11

MT MAJOR

TO ALTON

trail. Wild cherries, pines, young white birch, and mountain maple extend into the blueberry patches. The trail reaches the final ledges. These are at first sharp and in places sheer for a few feet, putting you to handholds and careful footholds. This is scrambling, not rock climbing. The upper ledges are worn by glaciers and by exposure, but the coarse, notched surfaces are readily surmounted. On the open summit, a four-sided stone shelter stands out against the sky. Roofless, its rock slabs, mortared into walls, were built in 1925 by George M. Phippen, a lifelong summer resident of Alton Bay. Winter winds took off two roofs. From this landmark various outlooks open in all directions. The views sweep around you, but the lake catches and holds your attention.

Long and narrow, Alton Bay extends to the south. Northward the big lake stretches to the east shore and the town of Wolfeboro. Directly north is the length of Rattlesnake Island. Beyond, the blue

water extends northwesterly broken by many islands and peninsulas, or "necks," which blend in the distance with the reaches of the lake and wooded slopes rising to the Sandwich Range and Ossipee Mountains. Often in summer, haze obscures the farther peaks, but on a day of real clarity you can see Mount Moosilauke, the tips of one or two Franconias, Sandwich Mountain, Whiteface, Passaconaway, and—rising behind Ossipee's long ridge—Mount Washington. To the west, Belknap Mountain's tower marks that summit, above lesser, forested ridges.

Mount Major, open rock except for blueberry bushes and small birches, exposes you to cooling breezes, welcome after the climb.

Descend by the same route.

14

Stinson Mountain

Distance (round trip): 3½ miles
Walking time: 2 hours
Vertical rise: 1,390 feet
Map: USGS 7½' Rumney

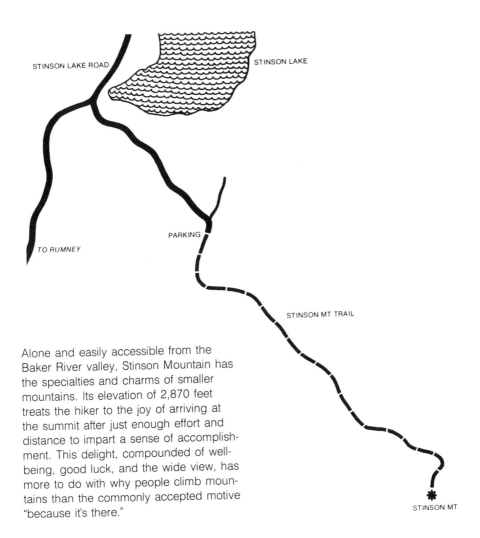

Alone and easily accessible from the Baker River valley, Stinson Mountain has the specialties and charms of smaller mountains. Its elevation of 2,870 feet treats the hiker to the joy of arriving at the summit after just enough effort and distance to impart a sense of accomplishment. This delight, compounded of well-being, good luck, and the wide view, has more to do with why people climb mountains than the commonly accepted motive "because it's there."

Trillium

The summit ledges, once the site of a fire tower, offer fine views. Forests, mountains, and lakes surround the lovely rural valley along Baker River with its farms and houses. The Franconia Range and the Sandwich Range are north and east. The village of Rumney lies at the foot of the mountain, Stinson Lake in the hollow to the north, Campton Bog to the east. Lesser-known mountains on the west—Mount Cube, Smarts Mountain, Piermont Mountain, Carr Mountain—are clothed in forests. To the north, Mount Moosilauke rises above treeline.

Pleasant and varied in any season from spring to late fall, Stinson Mountain is especially fine in October, not only for the trail, which rises through leafed woods of red and yellow, but for the blends of colors spreading out in all directions from the summit. By then the cone of Mount Moosilauke is sometimes snowcapped.

Drive west from Plymouth on NH 25 to Rumney. Turn north through the village to Stinson Lake. Bear right near the outlet of the lake and continue uphill to a sharp left turn. Swing to the right onto a road less traveled and across a small bridge. Drive .3 mile to parking on the left at the start of the Stinson Mountain Trail.

The path leads into open woods and along stone walls to an old cellar hole, which it passes on a left corner. Large trees grow from the cellar, demonstrating the many years since (probably) the roof of the farmhouse fell in after the family moved west or became city folks.

The trail ascends gradually to a trickling brook, which cannot be counted on for water in dry seasons. Here you begin the real climb by turning right and going up the steep slope. Alternately switching from steep grades to easier old logging roads, the trail passes a narrow opening with a view over Stinson Lake and toward Mount Moosilauke. Entering spruce and fir woods interspersed with striped maple and mountain ash for the last climb, the trail curves right and breaks out all at once into the clearing at the ledges.

15

Mount Cardigan

Distance (around the loop): 3½ miles
Walking time: 2½ hours
Vertical rise: 1,220 feet
Map: USGS 15′ Cardigan

A crown of solid rock forms the top of Mount Cardigan. As you approach the fire tower lookout exposed to the open sky and wind, you are taken by the illusion of climbing on the barren rock of some remote and mightier mountain; instead you are on an outpost of the White Mountains at only 3,121 feet elevation. The illusion is dispelled by the sight of initials and dates carved in the rock over the years. Cardigan has been a popular climb for a long time, and many trails ascend it.

The route of this hike is a loop from the Cardigan State Reservation's parking and picnic area up the West Ridge Trail, and return via South Peak and the South Ridge Trail. Access roads approach through the towns west of the mountain, Canaan and Orange.

Cardigan's distinctive rock dome is extended by the lower ledges of the north and south ridges. The rock is known as Cardigan pluton. It is a form of Kinsman quartz monzonite common in New Hampshire and is part of a formation at various levels, sixty miles long and twelve miles wide, extending from West Peterborough to north of Groton.

Here on Cardigan, forest fires destroyed the trees and organic earth, and erosion exposed the bare rock. In

1855, a fire twisted up in flame and smoke from the north ridge so spectacularly and with such destruction that the rock is still largely barren, and the ridge is named "Firescrew," from the spiraling smoke and flames that were visible in all the villages for miles around.

The south ridge is also open rock, with only scattered evergreens. Views from South Peak are mostly east and west. But pick a clear day. Summer haze, which spoils the view, can sometimes be avoided by making an early morning climb.

About the first week in May, the lower forested slopes of hardwoods show the greenery of new leaves while trees above are still bare or only budded. In the fall, the first yellow and red leaves appear near the summit, while the lower trees remain green. Changes requiring weeks at a single elevation appear in one glance down the mountainside.

Also, in spring and fall, watch out for ice on the rock. You could slide a long way into the trees with time to think about other errors before the crash.

Growing below the South Peak's ridge in May will be dogtooth violets—really members of the lily family—and small yellow violets, purple trillium, and wood anemone. In summer look for the flat

On Mt. Cardigan

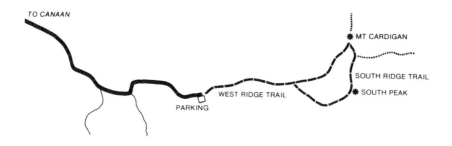

leaves of the green-flowered orchis.

Binoculars are useful to study the lakes and farther ranges, or to peer into towns, or to watch a raven near the summit. This bird from the north has been seen recently on Cardigan. Warblers flock to the wooded slopes at migration time.

The summit receives the full blast of the wind. Before the closing of New Hampshire towers, a climb to the lookout gave you an unbelievable "ride." The glassed-in room seemed to rush downward with a rocking, roaring rumble, straining against the cables. In a high wind, the room sounded and felt like a subway car.

The view, starting west and looking counterclockwise, extends to Vermont, then Massachusetts, then east over the New Hampshire Lakes Region and the Belknaps, and around to the northeast, where the Sandwich Range is moored by the pinnacle of Mount Chocorua. Perhaps clouds swirl over the distant Presidentials and Franconias. Mount Moosilauke, northward, may be impressively white in early spring and late fall. To the northwest where four townships meet by Bryant Pond, a ridge running south is scarred by old mica mines.

To reach the west side of the mountain and the West Ridge Trail, drive to Canaan on US 4. Turn north on NH 118, and soon take a right on the road to Orange. Beyond the town hall and school, which are on the left, continue straight, over the bridge spanning

Orange Brook. The road forks. Keep right, on the Grafton Road, for about .8 mile to another fork. Turn left up to the entrance to Cardigan State Park and the .5 mile of road leading to the parking area and picnic tables.

The West Ridge Trail leaves the picnic clearing at a sign on the edge of the woods and climbs by easy stages, passing two springs in the first ¾ mile. Keep left past the South Ridge Trail, which offers the best views as part of the return loop. Above this junction, a short, side climb leads to outlooks to the right and then rejoins the main West Ridge Trail. Walk past the Skyland Trail, which is a ridge route to Alexandria Four Corners. Watch ahead frequently for the trail's blazes; especially keep a sharp eye open when you approach one of the numerous branching paths that are *not* your route.

The West Ridge Trail crosses a footbridge, leads past an open-front shelter, passes two branch trails, and ascends steeply over rock, along a route identified by cairns and white paint, to the lookout tower.

In descending, go down to the lookout's cabin, bear right from the junction with the Clark Trail, and take the South Ridge Trail. This leads you over partially wooded ledges beyond South Peak with its great views, to Rimrock, then crosses Skyland Trail, and slabs around through woods to the West Ridge Trail at the junction you passed on the way up, about ¾ mile above the parking area.

Franconia
Notch Region

After twenty years of opposition by conservationists to extending I-93 through the notch, we have a compromise parkway nearing completion at this writing (fall 1985). Trailheads have changed, there are new visitor centers for the Flume and the Profile, new parking arrangements, and a bicycle path through the woods parallel to the parkway.

The following list gives you available directions. Remember that you can ask at the information booth, Lafayette Place, east of the parkway.

#17 Mount Pemigewasset. Construction; check for new start.

#18 Basin-Cascades Trail. Check.

#19 Lonesome Lake. No change.

#20 and #21. Mount Flume and Mount Liberty. The parkway goes through the former parking lot at White House Bridge. New parking is to the north. From this area take bicycle path south. The Liberty Spring Trail diverges from the bicycle path east of the new bridge. The AMC has placed signs.

#22 Mount Lincoln. The Old Bridle Path and Falling Waters Trail leave the new parking east of Lafayette Place and coincide for ¼ mile. At the bridge over Walker Brook, they divide. Turn right across the bridge for Falling Waters Trail. The Old Bridle Path is relocated for a section straight ahead.

#23 Mount Lafayette. Greenleaf Trail start is under construction; check.

#24 North Lafayette. At present unaffected. Eventually the exit off I-93 will be different.

#25 Cannon Mountain. The Kinsman Ridge Trail, basically unchanged except the first few yards, leaves the road to the new visitor center for the Profile. Return from Lafayette Place is now the bicycle path, reached as described for Profile Lake Trail.

Maps for these hikes are unchanged and may reflect former trailhead locations.

View from Artist Bluff

16

Artist Bluff and Bald Mountain

Distance (round trip): 1½ miles
Walking time: 1¼ hours
Vertical rise: 400 feet
Map: USGS 7½′ Franconia

Franconia Notch with its state park and famous Profile, two lakes, the Tramway, and ski trails, all bordering US 3, has too many attractions for a quick visit. Don't try to see all the lakes, streams, precipices, and rock formations in a day. Along with Cannon Mountain, Eagle Cliff, and Mount Lafayette, they are overpowering. First, get a hiker's perspective. If time is short and the urge to escape speeding cars and wandering tourists is imperative, climb Artist Bluff and Bald Mountain at the north end of the Notch. You need only an hour or two.

Stop and look at the Profile—New Hampshire's unique "Old Man of the Mountains." Then drive north on US 3

past the Tramway and its cable cars up Cannon Mountain. Keep Echo Lake on your left. At the end of the lake turn left onto NH 18, which soon brings you to the parking area for Echo Lake Beach. Leave your car there.

The trail to Artist Bluff starts on the north side of NH 18. Walk back east from the parking area. The trail is on your left near a highway route sign and west of the outlet from Echo Lake. Climb the highway embankment by a path worn in the gravel. At a sign for the bluff the trail enters the woods and leads up among big rocks. There's a steep climb up a gully.

Near the top, you turn right on a spur trail a few yards to Artist Bluff. This is a rock cliff from which artists might paint the Notch, but it's more often a vantage point for photographers. The view is magnificent across Echo Lake to Eagle Cliff and Mount Lafayette, left, and to Cannon Mountain on the right.

For a complete hike above the north and western gateways of the Notch, return to the trail and turn right. Climb the remainder of the gully and over the wooded height above. The trail leads up and down over the knolls. You pass another ledge lookoff before you de-scend to the sag below Bald Mountain's summit. Watch for the tall old spruces along the trail. Most of them have been struck by lightning, and their trunks bear the vertical scars. The trail joins a former carriage road up from NH 18. Turn right for Bald Mountain. Climb the trail by a series of steps over rock from the first switchback.

On the rocky open summit you stand clear of the small spruces. You look west over Franconia village, far away to the Connecticut River valley, and into Vermont. Cannon Mountain's ski slopes are south. Turning around left, you look into the deep Notch, again across Echo Lake.

Return to the junction with the Artist Bluff Trail. Turn right and follow the trail down the graded, ancient carriage road to NH 18. It ends at the parking area for skiers on the Roland Peabody Memorial Slope. Keep left across the parking area and walk beside NH 18 back to the Echo Lake Beach parking area.

17

Mount Pemigewasset

Distance (round trip): 2½ miles
Walking time: 2 hours
Vertical rise: 1,150 feet
Map: USGS 7½' Lincoln

Mount Pemigewasset, at the south end of Franconia Notch, is the buttress for the Indian Head, whose impassive profile looks down upon the motels and restaurants along US 3 north of North Woodstock. It is also a summit with extensive views. The mountain extends north from the cliffs forming the Indian Head, and the trail to the summit from that direction starts opposite the entrance to the Flume. The open ledges at the end of the climb give the mountain an individuality that is more spectacular than its height would suggest, for its elevation is only 2,554 feet, less than half that of Mount Lafayette five miles away to the northeast.

After the tourist attractions of the Notch, you'll be refreshed by this climb above the highway and by the view of

the mountains or down the valley. At sunset, you watch the horizon glow, and you are treated to a much rarer sight: the low-angled shadows and the brilliancy of late sun on the peaks of the Notch, a series of gleaming crests above the purple valley.

It will be time then to return the 1¼ miles to the highway and your car. For a

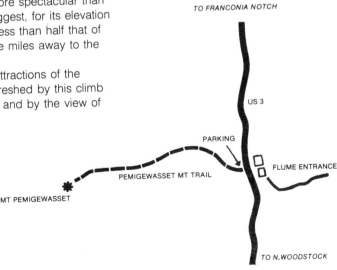

On the Pemigewasset Mountain Trail

sunset hike, take a flashlight with new batteries and a picnic supper in a small knapsack. If you linger on the mountain, you will find that the twilight of the summit has changed to darkness down by US 3.

In the days of mountain inns, instead of returning to a parked car, you would have crossed a lawn to the lights and hospitality of the Flume House.

To reach the trail, park on the west side of US 3, across from the Flume buildings. The Pemigewasset Mountain Trail starts at the south end of the parking area. It crosses a small open picnic space, and, at the upper left, enters the woods as an improved path. After ½ mile, this path joins a much older trail and swings left, upward along that route, then above a small brook, which the trail meets but does not cross. It turns sharply right up a bank. A steady climb takes you to the north side of the mountain and the beginning of spruce and fir growing among the hardwoods. The trail leads on to the broad ledges above the cliffs at the summit.

18

Basin-Cascades Trail

Distance (to Cascade Brook Trail and back): 3 miles
Walking time: 2 hours
Vertical rise: 500 feet
Maps: USGS 7½' Lincoln; USGS 7½' Franconia

Of the various trails maintained in the Notch by the New Hampshire Division of Parks, the Basin-Cascades Trail is one of the most interesting. It passes through woods of fine stature and it climbs up beside falls, pools, and rock formations along the way.

The Basin-Cascades Trail may be considered a link from the Basin to Cascade Brook Trail, which leads on to Lonesome Lake, but for hikers exploring the Notch it is an experience in itself for an afternoon in mountain woods.

North of the Flume about 1.5 miles, the old road through the Notch has been preserved to the west of US 3 and gives access to the big glacial pothole called the Basin. There are parking places and picnic tables.

To reach the Basin-Cascades Trail, cross the footbridge at the Basin and another over a tributary to the Pemigewasset River. The path beyond that will soon be joined by the Pemi-Trail coming down from Lafayette Campground. (The Pemi-Trail and the Profile Lake Trail north of Lafayette Campground make it possible to walk about four miles along the Pemigewasset River, with easy grades and footbridges, between the Basin and Profile Lake.)

At the junction with the Pemi-Trail, the Basin-Cascades Trail bears left toward Cascade Brook. Recently no trail signs have identified these paths. Don't take one branching left downstream. Keep walking up past the way to a footbridge on your right. A few yards farther, you'll pass another trail on your right, the Pemi-Trail, into a little hollow and up a bank. Keep straight ahead for the Basin-Cascades Trail. It soon begins to angle left. You climb to the ridge above the brook. For your first breathing pause you'll see the water sliding over smooth ledges.

The trail follows the north bank past cascades and past Kinsman Falls. Various spur trails on the left offer better views than the main trail. Above the falls, the trail crosses the brook on a bridge consisting of a single log and hand rail. This sometimes deters casual adult walkers, and certainly should turn back families with small children.

Beyond the bridge the trail climbs steeply and continues to follow the brook through evergreen woods. Scrambling in places is necessary. You pass between two rock dikes. Tree roots have been exposed by erosion and boots. The spruces shadow the brook so that Rocky

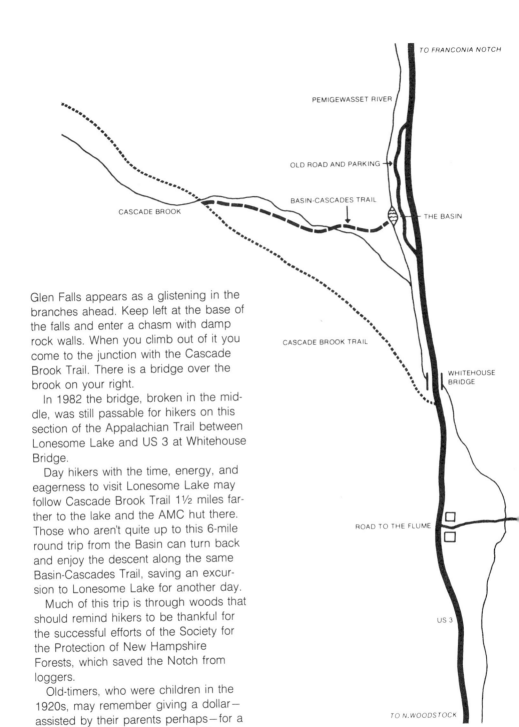

TO FRANCONIA NOTCH

PEMIGEWASSET RIVER

OLD ROAD AND PARKING

BASIN-CASCADES TRAIL

CASCADE BROOK

THE BASIN

CASCADE BROOK TRAIL

WHITEHOUSE BRIDGE

ROAD TO THE FLUME

US 3

TO N.WOODSTOCK

Glen Falls appears as a glistening in the branches ahead. Keep left at the base of the falls and enter a chasm with damp rock walls. When you climb out of it you come to the junction with the Cascade Brook Trail. There is a bridge over the brook on your right.

In 1982 the bridge, broken in the middle, was still passable for hikers on this section of the Appalachian Trail between Lonesome Lake and US 3 at Whitehouse Bridge.

Day hikers with the time, energy, and eagerness to visit Lonesome Lake may follow Cascade Brook Trail 1½ miles farther to the lake and the AMC hut there. Those who aren't quite up to this 6-mile round trip from the Basin can turn back and enjoy the descent along the same Basin-Cascades Trail, saving an excursion to Lonesome Lake for another day.

Much of this trip is through woods that should remind hikers to be thankful for the successful efforts of the Society for the Protection of New Hampshire Forests, which saved the Notch from loggers.

Old-timers, who were children in the 1920s, may remember giving a dollar—assisted by their parents perhaps—for a tree, in the Society's campaign, "Buy a

The Basin

Tree to Help Save the Notch." Major contributions came from philanthropists interested in conservation. Women's clubs, newspapers, and the Appalachian Mountain Club also contributed, as did the New Hampshire taxpayers through their legislature, which appropriated half the $400,000 required to buy the 6,000 acres along seven miles of US 3. Dedication ceremonies were held on September 15, 1928, at Profile Lake below the "Old Man of the Mountains." Dedication was to the New Hampshire men and women who had served the nation in time of war.

The Notch needed saving again in the 1970s when highway promoters planned to blast through it with I-93 and multiple lanes. The Society again led the fight to save the Notch and, with the AMC and a conservationist coalition, took their case to the federal courts. After an injunction, a compromise was worked out to improve US 3 as a parkway that would facilitate both traffic and tourist enjoyment through this splendid and historic pass in the White Mountains.

19

Lonesome Lake

Distance (round trip): 3¼ miles
Walking time: 2¾ hours
Vertical rise: 1,000 feet
Map: USGS 7½′ Franconia

One thousand feet above Franconia Notch is Lonesome Lake, a goal for climbers and visitors who take advantage of the graded trail to walk in and see a true mountain lake in a spectacular setting. No longer "lonesome," quite the opposite, the much-used trails, along with the plywood hut of the AMC, and the voices of hikers with their colorful packs and clothes, give a modern touch to the ancient scenery.

The lake has been popular since the days of mountain inns after the Civil War. The trail still mostly follows the old bridle path, along which many vacationers from the now-vanished hotels rode to the lake for the magnificent views of the mountains on both sides of the Notch.

Legend names President Ulysses S. Grant as one of the notable visitors. According to the story, he came to the Notch and the Profile House in 1869. A yellow coach and six bay horses driven by Ed Cox, a famous "whip," brought him from Bethlehem in fifty-five minutes—a fantastic rate of more than thirteen miles an hour. In later years, a steam train and rails brought guests to the Profile House, which burned in August 1923.

The views from Lonesome Lake are, indeed, great—comprehensive, craggy,

wild, and dominated by the treeless peak of Mount Lafayette. From the lake, trails lead to Cannon Mountain, Mount Kinsman, and Kinsman Pond. The Appalachian Trail passes by the lower end of the lake.

As many as forty-six hikers can be accommodated at the AMC's Lonesome Lake Hut, situated on the west shore facing the Franconia Range. There is a trail around the lake, ¾ mile, passing the site of old log cabins. A stand of tamarack makes a fine display of yellow in the fall. The lake is 2,734 feet above sea level. Westward, the evergreen forest rises to the ledges of Mount Kinsman.

Park at Lafayette Place. This is a clearing, picnic area, and campground between the Profile and the Flume on the west side of US 3. When you leave your car, pause and walk around until you can see the best view of the cliffs of Cannon Mountain.

The Lonesome Lake Trail will be found by walking beyond the picnic area. Near the south end is a stream that's already called by its full name, Pemigewasset River. Cross this on the footbridge. Walk through the campground following yellow trail blazes to the entrance into the woods. Very shortly, the trail begins the

Lonesome Lake

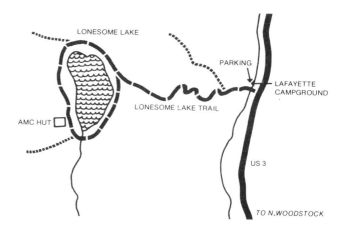

series of graded switchbacks up the steep slope.

You surmount most of the 1,000 feet to the lake in the ridge's first ½ mile. You work your way upward by the switchbacks originally designed for horses and riders, but now equally useful to hikers. Pass by the Hi-Cannon Trail on the right. The Lonesome Lake Trail continues to climb. The ridge, which looked so easy from Lafayette Place, seems to have deceived you. But the trail soon begins to level out, and, after about 1 mile, you detect a slight descent. The lake is ahead in its flat wooded setting. You come to a trail junction. Pause here and study the trail sign and the numerous trails listed. Orient yourself to the map.

Even look behind you to familiarize yourself with the trail you've been on, so you'll recognize it when you return to it.

To reach the AMC hut, take the Cascade Brook Trail, which branches left from the Lonesome Lake Trail. Follow along the east shore of the lake until you come to another trail junction at the lake's south end. Turn right on the Fishin' Jimmy Trail across the outlet, and take the left fork to the AMC hut.

For the return route, walk the Around-Lonesome-Lake Trail on the west shore to a junction with the Lonesome Lake Trail north of the lake. Turn right. Keep past the Cascade Brook Trail, and you are on the way back down to Lafayette Place.

Mount Flume

Distance (round trip via Flume Slide Trail): 8 miles
  (round trip via Mount Liberty loop): 8¼ miles
Walking time (either way): 6½ hours
Vertical rise (Flume Slide Trail only): 2,927 feet
  (including Mount Liberty loop): 3,327 feet
Map: USGS 7½' Lincoln

Appearing as a rocky pinnacle to the drivers and passengers northbound on I-93 and US 3 into Woodstock, Mount Flume sets the style for the Franconia Range. This southern terminus of the long ridge above treeline is a fitting introduction to Mount Liberty, Mount Lincoln, and Mount Lafayette. But Mount Flume has its own distinction, namely, the slide, which you climb via the Flume Slide Trail.

Mount Flume overlooks the rock chasm and cascades near US 3 and the entrance to Franconia Notch, known to generations of sightseers as the Flume. Formerly, the Flume served hikers as an access route to trails up both Mount Flume and its northern neighbor, Mount Liberty. Trail relocation in 1972 moved the starting point for these climbs north to the Appalachian Trail crossing on US 3.

To reach the Flume Slide Trail, drive north from North Woodstock on US 3 past the Flume entrance. Proceed .8 mile to Whitehouse Bridge spanning the young Pemigewasset River. A sign identifies the Appalachian Trail where it comes out of the woods, left. Drive across the bridge. Turn right for parking, picnic tables, and trail signs.

Walking east across the parking area, you come to the beginning of the Liberty Spring Trail, which takes you up fairly steeply through the hardwoods less than half a mile to the Flume Slide Trail. Bear right at this fork. (The Liberty Spring Trail continues toward Liberty Spring Campsite and Mount Liberty.)

You begin the pleasant woods walk south and east for almost 3 miles to the base of the mountain. The trail follows a series of old logging roads and crosses various tributaries of Flume Brook. As you approach the base of the slide the trail can be altered annually by spring freshets. Watch for the blue blazes. This is the last water. The upper ridge is dry. It is also dangerous when closed in by clouds and rain, particularly during summer thunderstorms; then there is plenty of water in the form of rain, but a lightning bolt might end your climbing.

The challenge of Mount Flume begins at the slide. For more than ½ mile, you face the side of the mountain where once an avalanche of rocks and gravel poured down. Now somewhat grown to small birches and evergreens, it still keeps your eyes focused on footholds and handholds. Pause for the views opening across the Notch to Mount Kinsman and

Climbers on Franconia Ridge

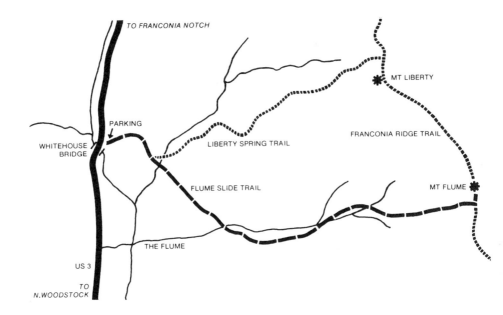

Cannon Mountain. Climbing here for those with packs is easier than descending—except for the demand on lungs—but caution is required either way. Double your care if rain has soaked the rocks.

At the top of the slide keep left as the trail enters spruces and firs, climbing to the junction with the Franconia Ridge Trail. At the right, the Osseo Trail leads south over wooded Osseo Peak to the Kancamagus Highway almost six miles away.

Follow the Franconia Ridge Trail left up into the spruce scrub to the edge of the open cliffs above the slide you have climbed. A few yards to the north is the summit of the peak, a small area of rock. The effect is immediate—a sense of achievement and emergence from a hard climb to an extreme height. Elevation, 4,327 feet. The view is grand in all directions.

Northward, you see the barren and rocky crests of Mount Liberty, Mount Lincoln, and Mount Lafayette, highest in the range. Turning west, you look across the

Notch to the humped summits of Mount Kinsman, and, at the head of the Notch, Cannon Mountain bulking above the Profile's cliffs, which show no indication of the silhouette. To the east, your eyes sweep over the forested valleys draining into the Pemigewasset River's East Branch. The far ridge in this Pemigewasset "Wilderness" rises north from cilffs to Mount Bond's treeless summit. Mount Carrigain, farther east, bounds the "Wilderness" with its massive pyramid topped by an observation tower.

If the afternoon is only beginning and the weather remains fine, you can yield to the appeal of another summit, Mount Liberty, down and up 1¼ miles north along the Franconia Ridge Trail. Beyond the peak, turn left down the Liberty Spring Trail for completion of a loop back to your car.

But Mount Liberty is a good climb by itself. Save it for another day unless your vacation is running out. Return down the Flume Slide Trail, as you climbed, and watch your footing on the slide.

21

Mount Liberty

Distance (round trip): 6 miles
Walking time: 5 hours
Vertical rise: 3,060 feet
Map: USGS 7½′ Lincoln

The ledgy crest of Mount Liberty lines up with the higher Franconia Range northward and provides closer views of the Notch from a better angle than Mount Flume. Instead of a slide for a final approach, the Liberty Spring Trail leads up past a campsite popular with Appalachian Trail hikers.

The climb, like the one up Mount Flume (see Hike 20), begins at Whitehouse Bridge. Drive .8 mile up US 3 past the Flume entrance. The highway tops a hill and dips down to the bridge and to the parking area on the right, where you'll find trail signs and picnic tables.

The Liberty Spring Trail runs east out of the parking area. Climb ½ mile to the fork where Flume Slide Trail branches right. Keep left, as the Liberty Spring Trail continues up through the hardwood forest and crosses a brook.

Steadily rising, the trail takes you up slopes once logged and burned. In 1917, hikers climbing among rocks scorched bare by a forest fire followed signs nailed to blackened stubs.

The trail swings up steeply to your right, then becomes more gradual, and passes Liberty Spring Campsite. (No shelter here; tent platforms only. Last water.) On up through the spruce/fir woods you climb to the Franconia Ridge Trail. Turn right (south) and follow the Franconia Ridge Trail up into the open, where you see the steep rocky summit ahead. You feel that lift of excitement from the expanse of sky and mountain, and from the certainty that you'll soon surmount the last rocks.

This 4,460-foot peak overlooks the great forests to the east in the Pemigewasset "Wilderness." Northward, along the Franconia Ridge Trail, your gaze adjusts to the increasing height beyond Little Haystack Mountain, where narrow ledges rise to Mount Lincoln. On the left a distant green ridge curves down from AMC's Greenleaf Hut into the Notch below Mount Lafayette, which Mount Lincoln obscures. North, across the Notch, the high cliffs of Cannon Mountain appear chopped from the wooded summit. Westward, Mount Kinsman's slope and long, summit ridge parallel the highway. In the opposite direction, east, Owl's Head, more like a great whale, fills the valley north toward Mount Garfield. Over Owl's Head, past Mount Guyot, the peak on the northeastern horizon is Mount Washington. And all around, distant under a clear sky and high clouds, the mountains seem endless.

Mt. Liberty

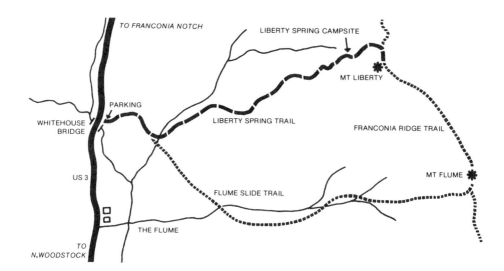

Often, however, Mount Liberty is in cloud, and the wind is cold. But luck favors the prepared hiker; if you carry, in a pack, plenty of extra clothing and rain parka, maybe you won't need them; then you can sit in the sun and enjoy your sandwiches and Liberty Spring water from your canteen.

The descent takes you north along the Franconia Ridge Trail on the same route you climbed. Turn left onto the Liberty Spring Trail, which you follow back to your car.

22

Mount Lincoln

Distance (round trip, Mount Lincoln only): 7 miles
(around the loop, Lincoln and Lafayette): 8 miles
Walking time (Mount Lincoln only): 5¾ hours
(around the loop): 7½ hours
Vertical rise (to Mount Lincoln): 3,350 feet
(around the loop): 3,750 feet*
Map: USGS 7½' Franconia

To many hikers along the Franconia Ridge Trail, Mount Lincoln is a way station on the high line of peaks knifing north and south above Franconia Notch east of US 3. But Mount Lincoln can be a fine destination in itself. During the ascent, you will see spectacular waterfalls, a unique slanting cliff, alpine-arctic environment above treeline, and wide, wide views, especially overlooking the Pemigewasset "Wilderness" clear away to Crawford Notch and Mount Washington. This hike offers the added bonus of a climb up the highest peak in the Franconia Range, Mount Lafayette, if you wish.

Leave your car at Lafayette Place two miles south of the Tramway on the west side of US 3, where the state of New Hampshire maintains a picnic area and campground. Cross the highway. Walk around a gate and past the AMC Information Booth. Bear right to the Falling Waters Trail.

* Mount Lafayette is only 141 feet higher than Mount Lincoln, but the climb from the col north of Mount Lincoln is 400 feet.

In the first ½ mile, you cross Walker Brook flowing from a ravine on Mount Lafayette, and you ascend gradually, swinging through woods of maple, beech, and yellow birch, for another ½ mile to Dry Brook. Contrary to its name, the brook is a crystal torrent in early summer.

You cross Dry Brook to the south bank and begin a steeper climb. You pass cascades on the left and approach ledges high up in the trees. The trail appears to end at a pool in a narrow ravine. Swiftwater Falls gushes into the pool from a ledge sixty feet high. You see the trail to the left of the falls. You cross to the opposite bank over rocks at the foot of the pool.

The climb begins here in earnest, although the trail is graded, and sections of it follow old logging roads. You were impressed by Swiftwater Falls. Now Cloudland Falls, twenty feet higher, descends toward you in a white, shifting curtain sliding into the gorge.

Above Cloudland Falls, from the steep and slippery ledge, you first look out across the valley. Keep to the north

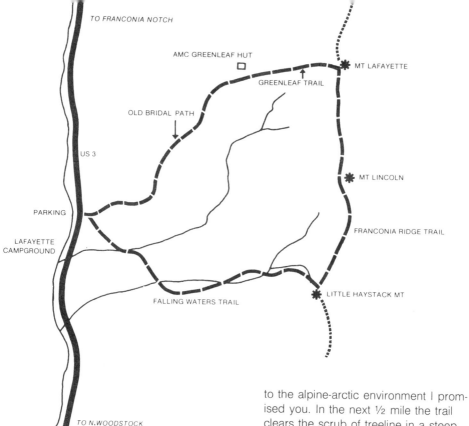

TO FRANCONIA NOTCH

AMC GREENLEAF HUT

GREENLEAF TRAIL

MT LAFAYETTE

OLD BRIDAL PATH

US 3

MT LINCOLN

PARKING

FRANCONIA RIDGE TRAIL

LAFAYETTE
CAMPGROUND

LITTLE HAYSTACK MT

FALLING WATERS TRAIL

TO N.WOODSTOCK

bank. The trail continues up rough and steep as the brook branches into the upper growth of spruce and fir. The trail takes you up a series of traverses between steeper pitches to a left turn at a junction. Here a sign indicates the spur trail 100 yards to the right, which leads down to the base of Shining Rock Cliff. This massive expanse of smooth granite angles up at a rounded forty-five degrees for 200 feet to your left. It extends four times that across the ridge. It gleams in the sun when wet from the drainage off its brow of evergreens. Don't try to climb it. From your parked car at Lafayette Place in late afternoon you can see it really shining.

Back at the junction with the main trail you may wonder how much farther it is to the alpine-arctic environment I promised you. In the next ½ mile the trail clears the scrub of treeline in a steep ascent into the open rockery of Little Haystack, a minor peak on the Franconia Ridge Trail.

If the wind blows rain, and clouds are settling into a blinding fog, this is a good place to turn back. Wait for a better day. The exciting panorama from the ridge demands a clear view. There's no value in a memory of Mount Lincoln as gray rocks packed in cotton batting. Besides, the ridge is dangerous in stormy weather. Lightning strikes frequently. Winds can be icy even in summer. You will be almost a mile up in the sky. The col between Little Haystack and Mount Lincoln is exposed, narrow, and in places almost sheer on each side.

In fine weather, turn north along the Franconia Ridge Trail and enjoy the ¾ mile above trees in the open exposure of sun and sky. The summit of Mount Lincoln is at 5,108 feet.

Mt. Lincoln

Multiplicities of mountains rise in all directions, and on the east the rocks fall away to green forests along Lincoln Brook and Franconia Branch, which flow around 4,023-foot Owl's Head anchored like a humped barge in the green sea of trees.

For a loop and return to your car, the Franconia Ridge Trail provides a clear-day bonus beyond Mount Lincoln. North, beyond Mount Lincoln's summit, the trail descends, down, over, and among rocks, all in the open, then up to Mount Lafayette's rugged slopes and summit cairn — a 1-mile hike among alpine-arctic plants, such as diapensia, hugging the windswept ledges. From Mount Lafayette turn left and go down by the Greenleaf Trail to the AMC's Greenleaf Hut. Then take the Old Bridle Path for the descent along a ridge where, in June, the rhodora blossoms are showy pink above Walker Ravine. The Old Bridle Path takes you to your starting point opposite Lafayette Place. If you don't choose to include the loop to Mount Lafayette, you may return from Mount Lincoln as you climbed and enjoy once again Shining Rock Cliff, Cloudland Falls, and Swiftwater Falls.

23

Mount Lafayette

Distance (round trip): 7 miles
Walking time: 6 hours
Vertical rise: 3,475 feet
Map: USGS 7½' Franconia

The "top of the world" in the Franconia Range is, of course, named for the French hero of the American Revolution. His 1825 visit to New Hampshire brought about the change from the peak's older name of Great Haystack. Its northwestern cliffs and slides form the east side of Franconia Notch above Profile Lake. Its long, forested slopes of beech and yellow birch rise above US 3 for two miles southward. Far up among the spruce scrub and barren rocks of treeline are two small lakes and the Greenleaf Hut of the AMC. The dwarf trees and ledges extend to a rock-strewn slope, 1 mile long, leading up to the summit at 5,249 feet, with rare mosses, plants, lichens, and grasses along the way.

The exposed stones of the peak could be arctic rather than in the temperate zone. Even on a summer day the wind often blows bitter cold. Plants are balanced on a delicate ecological margin. The dwarf spruces lie down before the wind and seem to grasp the rocks. Although doused with rain and fog, the mountain cranberry and similar creeping plants are thick-leaved against dehydration from the wind. The leaves of the low shrub, Labrador tea, curl along the edges and are woolly underneath, there-by retarding evaporation of vital leaf moisture in the harsh winds. These mountain vines, prostrate bushes, and shrubby heaths blossom white, pink, and purple in early summer.

Mount Lafayette has long been a popular climb. The oldest trail, still called the Old Bridle Path, was more than a name once. Travelers rode up it on mountain ponies from the Lafayette House, which burned in 1861. Only foundation stones remain of the vanished summit house, too, which in those days accommodated the successful climbers.

When the AMC built Greenleaf Hut, burros bore loads up the path and each year continued to transport supplies early in the season. Then, before the days of helicopters, the regular summer packing of necessary food and fuel depended on the legs and lungs of the hutmen lugging the long packboards. Still today, you will see hutmen treading upwards under heavy loads.

The Old Bridle Path, leaving US 3 from the east side at Lafayette Place, is the scenic route up Lafayette. The views of the upper ridge and of Walker Ravine open out from a partially wooded shoulder halfway up to Greenleaf Hut. Starting as it does at the same point as the Falling Waters Trail, described in the Mount Lincoln climb, the Old Bridle Path forms a pleasant and easy link in that loop. (See Hike 22.)

A northerly and more challenging route from Franconia Notch up Mount Lafayette, the Greenleaf Trail, mounts beside Eagle Cliff and reaches the north slope through Eagle Pass, 1,000 feet above the Notch, and opposite the Profile.

Park at the area east of US 3, 10 miles north of North Woodstock, used by tourists who stop to view the profile of the Old Man. Walk north to the bank above the highway and beyond the parking area. A few cars are usually parked there where the Greenleaf Trail begins. Don't let the graded path, the footbridge crossing between two ponds, or the nature trail stations deceive you into thinking this is not a rugged mountain trail. The Greenleaf Trail, blazed with blue paint, parallels US 3 through open woods, and then strikes up the steep slope by a series of switchbacks. The footing is excellent and continues so on the upper trail as it curves north into Eagle Pass. You enter the pass under a long cliff similar to those towering still higher above. You pick your way over massive rocks as large as cottages, which have lodged in the pass. Snow and ice linger late in the gloomy caves below the boulders. If you leave the trail to explore, watch out for treacherous patches of moss over the crevices. The trail itself is safe enough.

Beyond the rocky confines of Eagle Pass, the trail turns sharply right, south, on a side-hill slope and attacks the bulk of Mount Lafayette's north shoulder. The trail is steep and noted for its treacherous footing on loose stones. The trail rises at a lesser angle as it approaches the little flat before Greenleaf Hut and leads out of the evergreen scrub to the open views and challenging barrens above treeline. The glacial age is long gone, but the ice scoured the rocks before it melted away, leaving the great shards scattered precariously, a random and extravagant use of paving stone for men to wonder at.

Near the hut, the Old Bridle Path joins the Greenleaf Trail. You descend beyond the hut to the dwarf spruces again, then pass through the moist section at the little bog draining from the two basins of the

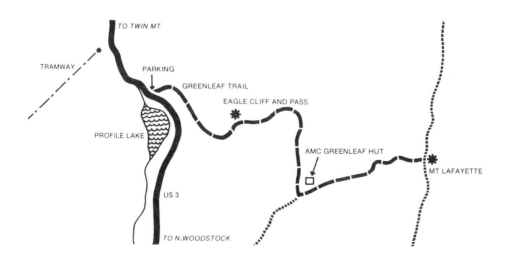

View of Mt. Lafayette

Eagle Lakes. You climb above tree line once more and follow the worn pathway over the rocks. Massive cairns mark the route, which swings north for the final ascent.

If there's a storm brewing, turn around and leave the mountain to the lightning and thunder. (In 1970, two young men camping overnight at the summit were almost killed by lightning.) If there's a clear hour ahead, watch the high clouds and their shadows moving across the mountains. Don't try to count the peaks. There are too many. Look east at the miles of green trees, and remember that before the days of the National Forest the valleys were a blackened devastation of logged and burned ridges.

Return by the same route, the Greenleaf Trail, turning right, north, at the hut for the descent to Eagle Pass.

North Lafayette

Distance: 7¾ miles
Walking time: 6 hours
Vertical rise: 3,280 feet
Map: USGS 7½' Franconia

After you've surmounted (and recovered from?) the highest and most popular climbing summit in the Franconia Range, a very different day awaits you on its north shoulder. From a rocky dome, sometimes called North Lafayette, you'll gaze at Mount Lafayette to the south half a mile away, and in a rarely seen perspective across a wide bowl of rock slabs and talus. A remoteness from the crowd on Lafayette's barren summit will emphasize the vastness of the mountain. You may even savor a mood of detachment, of isolation, which is a bonus for climbing this peak.

Of course it's not really isolated. The Garfield Ridge Trail crosses it at an elevation of about 5,080 feet. (The Garfield Ridge Trail traverses north from Mount Lafayette to AMC's Galehead Hut, a difficult six and one-half miles of the AT.) This trail above treeline, with its white AT blazes, will be your final quarter-mile southward after 3½ miles up the Skookumchuck Trail from US 3.

Drive north through Franconia Notch. Pass Echo Lake on your left and the junction with NH 18 leading to Franconia village. You soon look across an expansive panorama to the northwest. Beyond this at a bridge over a deep ravine, far up to your right above treeline, Mount Lafayette and its north peak are briefly visible.

Drive on till US 3 bears right at the fork with I-93 to the left. Stay on US 3. A hundred yards north of this junction a highway sign on the right silhouettes the figure of a hiker and indicates the start of the Skookumchuck Trail. Turn right up a short, steep driveway to a small parking space. (Parking is also available west of US 3 at a lookoff before the junction with I-93.)

The Skookumchuck Trail begins at the south corner of the small parking area. From the Forest Service sign, it follows an old logging road through a fine growth of maples, beeches, and birches. Nearly level, it heads south and then runs east beside Skookumchuck Brook on your right. Dug from the sidehill to form a sled road at an easy grade, it once led across log corduroy and crude bridges over boggy sections and seasonal streams. Modern trail crews, in 1979, added boulders for stepping stones and several split log walkways. The bank on your left becomes higher and steeper as you walk up the valley.

About forty-five minutes from your car, the trail turns left away from the brook and goes at the steep bank. For 300 feet you climb on rock steps. Deep waterbars of logs and earth prevent erosion. At the top your legs cease straining as the trail becomes less demanding. You reach another grade, which remains from the days of horse-drawn logging sleds. Spruces begin to blend with the white birches. Another steep climb brings you to a little flat where a trickle of water drips from the slope on your right.

The trail bears right to the foot of another upward pitch—again with rock steps to aid you. More important, the small boulders hold the trail in place. You may wonder at their size because they sometimes require very high lifting of your boots, with knees approaching your chin. This is not due to a wry sense of humor among trail crews. The rocks must contain enough weight to hold them in the shallow earth.

At the top of the steps you begin a steady climb. Here the trail narrows but the waterbars are adequate and the footing is good and not too rocky. The trees grow smaller. Approaching treeline? Not so. After a green tunnel ten feet high, the larger birches reappear among

tall evergreens and mountain ash trees. Look up to your right in the open woods and you'll see North Lafayette. It's not as far away as it appears.

The trail becomes typical of older routes on steep ridges. Evergreen branches reach into the narrow, rocky track and brush against your arms and hips. You grasp here and there tough roots or corners of rocks. Several short levels alternate with abrupt upward rock-scrambles, till you leave behind the final stunted spruces and stand in the open at treeline. Cairns mark the way up to the junction with the Garfield Ridge Trail.

Turn right onto the Garfield Ridge Trail. Soon you are climbing between low walls that keep you from walking on the delicate alpine vegetation. You'll see cushions of diapensia. Mountain sand-wort blossoms white well into the late summer when the creeping mountain cranberry has formed red fruit in the rock crevices.

The trail rises more sharply toward the sky and the scattered crags of North Lafayette. The summit is only a quarter-mile plus a few yards from the Skookum-chuck Trail. It's a beautiful place for lunch—on a good day; cold winds and cloud can buffet it and smother it. No need to join the fair-weather crowd over there southward on Mount Lafayette. Those hikers seem in a different world from the quiet of North Lafayette.

If the day is one of unlimited visibility, your luck may also bring you the thrill of watching a sailplane glide silently over your aerie. A sailplane might circle over Cannon Mountain's famous tramway, past the cliffs forming the Old Man of the Mountains across Franconia Notch, and rise up on a thermal like a great white hawk.

After that, your return is an anticlimax, although pleasantly easy down the same route you climbed.

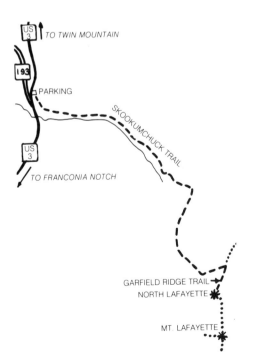

Cannon Mountain

Distance (round trip): 7¼ miles
Walking time: 5½ hours
Vertical rise: 2,100 feet
Map: USGS 7½' Franconia

You can ride in a Tramway cable car to the summit, so why climb Cannon Mountain on foot? Because only your two legs can make the mountain yours. Somehow this also improves the magnificent views of Franconia Notch and Mount Lafayette. For hikers aiming to climb all 4,000-footers, Cannon qualifies by 77 feet.

Skiers who have swooped down the snowy trails find that a summer climb, which pits them against this solid height unaided by Tramway or T-bars, gives the mountain new meaning.

A rounded block seen from the Notch, Cannon's stark cliffs loom before you as you drive north on US 3 toward the famous Profile. The mountain appears as a mass of stone on which evergreens cling with minimum success. Approach from the north, and you see its grassy ski slopes and trails like high pastures and giant paths down through the woods.

For a loop over the summit, climb the Kinsman Ridge Trail from the north and descend by the Hi-Cannon and Lonesome Lake Trails, returning through the Notch to your car via the Profile Lake Trail.

The Kinsman Ridge Trail begins its zig-zag climb about .3 mile south of the Tramway. Watch for an asphalt roadway

just south of the parking area west of US 3. Drive a few yards along this side road. Turn left onto a gravel track across a small field. Park at the edge of the woods.

This field, known as Profile Clearing, was the site of an immense old mountain hotel, the Profile House, which burned in 1923. From the field there's a view of the "cannon" that gave the mountain its name. If you walk to the field's center, turn around, and look west up the ridge in front of your car, you'll see a horizontal rock — the Cannon — outlined against the sky.

The Kinsman Ridge Trail climbs a bushy bank at the edge of the field a few yards south of a log cabin. At once you are on your way skyward. Steep for more than 1 mile, the trail gains altitude rapidly by a series of switchbacks. You climb to an opening in the trees and watch the cable cars slide gently up or down the black lines that suspend them.

As the trail angles away from the Tramway it becomes more difficult among rock slabs, which erosion has exposed. Watch out for your footing over roots and in gullies of rotten rock. Beyond this climb the trail levels out on the east shoulder. After a passage through small

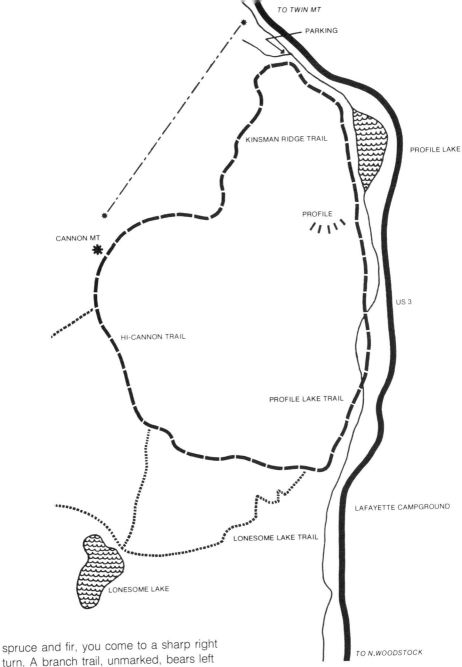

TO TWIN MT

PARKING

KINSMAN RIDGE TRAIL

PROFILE LAKE

PROFILE

CANNON MT

US 3

HI-CANNON TRAIL

PROFILE LAKE TRAIL

LAFAYETTE CAMPGROUND

LONESOME LAKE TRAIL

LONESOME LAKE

TO N.WOODSTOCK

spruce and fir, you come to a sharp right turn. A branch trail, unmarked, bears left to a breathtaking view from open ledges. North and south the Franconia crests line the horizon: Eagle Cliff, Mount Lafayette, Mount Lincoln, Little Haystack, and Mount Liberty.

On a ridge several hundred yards north, and from a camouflage of evergreen scrub, the Cannon aims at Mount Lafayette. From this angle it appears in its true form—a balanced rock

Cannon Mountain **97**

Cannon Mountain

shelf. You may wonder whether you're on the Profile's ledges. You're not. The Profile is dangerous, and reinforced rocks form the brooding silhouette far down and out of sight beyond the scrub and rocks.

Return to the main Kinsman Ridge Trail. Keep past the right turn leading back the way you came. The trail crosses the east shoulder, then dips into a wooded col. Soon you make a steep climb into the open again among rock slabs and alpine vegetation. All at once you hear voices and find yourself among people at the junction with the Rim Trail from the Tramway. A large sign names the peaks in the panorama. A short trail leads to the summit, and an observation tower puts you above the spruces. The Tramway terminal extends out from a niche, where ski trails begin to dive down.

Joining tourists at the tower, you look down the Notch and for an instant you are puzzled by a ribbon in the forest and toy cars. Across this highway, you see the Franconia Range, now part of a 360-degree view. Northward stretches the pastoral valley of the Gale River and Franconia village. South and west, a wilder panorama opens across Mount Kinsman's two summits toward Mount Moosilauke.

When you're ready to descend, return to the Kinsman Ridge Trail. Follow it where it passes southward below the summit from the junction where you turned up to the tower. (The trail continues its rugged way fifteen miles to its southern end at the Lost River Road in

Kinsman Notch.) Follow it only about ½ mile to the Hi-Cannon Trail where you turn left for the descent.

The Hi-Cannon Trail takes you past a lookoff ledge opening toward Mount Kinsman on your right and Lonesome Lake below you. The trail swings through young firs above cliffs from which there are wide outlooks into the Notch with its parallel ranges east and west. You climb down rocks on two short ladders and pass the eave-like ledges called Cliff House on your left.

Continue down a rough stretch into less precipitous woods. Keep left past the Dodge Cutoff which leads to Lonesome Lake. Hi-Cannon's switchbacks take you down to the Lonesome Lake Trail. Turn left and walk this graded path to Lafayette Campground. There, turn left and take the road out of the campground past the recreational building, Lafayette Lodge.

Follow the Profile Lake Trail that begins at the left just before the bridge out to the parking area. You have an interesting 2-mile hike north through the woods to the lake below the Profile. The mostly level trail crosses the Pemigewasset River on footbridges. Beavers have easily dammed the water, for it is only a brook, but they are gone now, and you can observe close at hand their gnawing technique on stumps. The trail rises to the lake. Keep left around the west side to the viewpoint for the Profile. Then walk north to the parking area and US 3, ¼ mile, and turn left into Profile Clearing where you parked your car.

Mount Kinsman

Distance (round trip): 10 miles
Walking time: 8 hours
Vertical rise: 3,400 feet
Maps: USGS 7½' Sugar Hill; USGS 7½' Franconia

Mount Kinsman has two summits. A wooded col and 1 mile of the Kinsman Ridge Trail connect them. The mountain forms a divide that separates the Merrimack River tributaries from the Connecticut River watershed to the west.

The north peak, elevation 4,275 feet, drops away 500 feet to narrow Kinsman Pond and the roof of the shelter near the spruce-grown shore. Beyond to the east, Lonesome Lake sparkles in the evergreen forest above Franconia Notch. Mount Lafayette, the giant of the region, rises across the Notch.

The south peak's dome, elevation 4,363 feet, because of topography and exposure, extends into the alpine-tundra zone above treeline, and provides views in all directions. From both summits, the Franconia Range outlines the eastern horizon. Sun and clouds endlessly shift lighting effects across the slopes.

Although hikers most often climb Mount Kinsman from Lonesome Lake, the route described here has the advantage of being less traveled and quite removed from the popularity of the Franconia Notch area. This hike takes you over both peaks and returns you by the same route. The Mount Kinsman Trail begins from the west in Easton, a township now grown back to woods from family farms of the nineteenth century. The Mount Kinsman Trail climbs to the Kinsman Ridge Trail, which traverses both summits.

Easton's settlement began at the conclusion of the Revolution. About 1783, Nathan Kinsman cut the first narrow woods-track into the wilderness territory that is now Easton. He brought in tools and supplies on six mules. He built a log cabin on his grant of six hundred acres. More settlers followed.

As in other mountain towns, the small meadows of Easton's valley and its rocky pastures fed and clothed an increasing population for seventy-five years until the Civil War. Then war casualties, hopes of easier western land, and cash wages from city industry drained away the young men. Now along NH 116, trees grow tall in the old farmland. The Mount Kinsman Trail crosses through some of this earlier farmland as it approaches the mountain's broad west slope. The trail begins on the east side of NH 116 seven miles north of Bungay Corner (on NH 112 west of Kinsman Notch). From the village of Franconia, the trail is 4 miles south on NH 116. Watch the mileage and go slowly or you'll miss the entrance

Mt. Kinsman, from Mt. Lafayette

road. It's identified by the highway's town line marker for Easton and Franconia. A gate and two large gateposts of laid-up stone bar the entrance to vehicles. Parking can be off to one side of the gate or along the highway shoulder.

The trail follows a bulldozed logging road through sandy cuts. It is badly washed out in places, and bordered by young spruces and birches growing up in the old pastures. The road becomes a wide path through a stand of maples near a sugar house.

Climbing more steeply, you approach a brook after 1½ miles. Cross the brook, bearing right, and climb up a steeper logging road. You will soon step over another brook with a mossy ledge on the left, then Flume Brook. A branch trail leads down to a ravine and cascade.

Shortly beyond Flume Brook, the main trail turns sharply left. A branch trail to the right leads to Bald Peak one-quarter mile through woods to wide views from rocks and blueberry bushes.

The main trail follows the dwindling brook. You look up at the steep ridge ahead. The trail rises steadily through spruces and firs. Golden-crowned kinglets, feeding in the upper branches, give notice of their presence only by faint cheeping notes and by small flutterings. But, if you look behind you on the steeper pitches, you can see the tiny birds in the treetops level with your eyes.

Among stunted evergreens you reach the Kinsman Ridge Trail. (This trail is a long, sixteen-mile trek over Cannon Mountain and Mount Kinsman to Kinsman Notch.) Turn right, south, on the

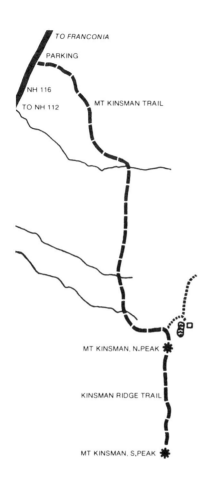

here, makes a narrow passage through evergreens and leads over rocky ledges to the north peak.

The north summit is partially wooded yet it offers a sudden view of Mount Lafayette, which becomes breathtaking from the cliff reached by a short trail left, east, down among rocks and spruces. The jagged Franconia Range cuts across the eastern horizon.

To continue, climb back up the spur trail to the Kinsman Ridge Trail. Turn left and continue south. You descend to the col and climb up out of the evergreens to the bare south dome and the summit cairn.

On several acres of open rock and dwarf spruces trimmed by the wind, you wander among abundant mountain plants, lichens, mosses, sedges, and grasses. In places, a matted turf has formed, held down by the roots of dwarf blueberry, Labrador tea, and mountain cranberry. Cool breezes and fine views make this the hike's ideal lunch setting.

In the afternoon, go back north along the Kinsman Ridge Trail over the north peak. Watch for the left turn into the Mount Kinsman Trail. Proceed down the Mount Kinsman Trail. Follow the route of your ascent, and remember not to be fooled at the corner where the Bald Peak spur trail invites you straight ahead; turn sharply right, down the straight logging road, then bear left across the brook.

Kinsman Ridge Trail. Take note of this junction so you'll recognize it on your return. The Kinsman Ridge Trail, along

27

Mount Moosilauke

Distance (round trip): 6 miles
Walking time: 5½ hours
Vertical rise: 2,400 feet
Maps: USGS 7½′ Mt. Kineo; USGS 7½′ Moosilauke

Rise early for Mount Moosilauke. It's a destination and an event. Bulking large on the southwestern border of the mountains, elevation 4,810 feet, massive and alone, its bare summit commands wide views in a complete circle.

The Franconias, fourteen miles northeast, march across the horizon. Far beyond them, Mount Washington appears with other Presidential peaks. More to the east, Mount Carrigain stands sentinel at the eastern approach to the Pemigewasset "Wilderness," which is bordered on the south by Mount Hancock, Osceola, Tripyramid, and the Sandwich Range. Directly south, smaller mountains scattered in the foothills blend toward isolated Mount Kearsarge (South) and Mount Cardigan. Westward, across the verdant Connecticut River valley, Vermont's Green Mountains extend as far as Killington Peak, Mount Mansfield, and Jay Peak.

Mount Moosilauke has been popular for more than a hundred years. In 1860, Sam Hoit built his stone Prospect House on the windswept summit. The opening ceremonies on the Fourth of July, according to one authority, attracted a thousand men and women. The gala crowd included a brass band, orators, militia,

and Indians. Refreshments were served. The Carriage Road continued to bring guests from Warren.

The Carriage Road was still safe for horse-drawn rigs in 1917. Dartmouth College took over the hotel in 1920 and put in bunks and accommodations for eighty hikers. In the summer, students managed the Summit House, or Tip-Top House as it was then called. Moosilauke has remained Dartmouth's mountain, although the Summit House burned in 1942. For a number of years the Dartmouth Outing Club maintained an emergency cabin below the summit, but by 1978 overuse and vandalism made its removal necessary. The college land is managed as a wilderness area where overnight camping and open fires are not permitted. This policy of limited use is designed to protect the unique and fragile mountain environment.

At all times the mountain can be cold and icy. Gales sweep down upon it with dangerous speed and intensity. Above treeline, clouds often shroud the rocks. The south shoulder, 1 mile long, is exposed to storms, and on a gloomy day suggests the beginning of the world despite the trail along the old Carriage Road traversing its length.

The trails starting near Dartmouth's Ravine Lodge offer the widest selection and most spectacular routes. Turn west off NH 118 between Warren and North Woodstock, 6 miles from Warren, onto the access road to the Lodge. Drive 1.5 miles to a turnaround. Head back along the road and park on the right-hand shoulder. With adequate clothing for this above-treeline climb, and of course food and water, walk to the left side of the turnaround, northwest, near a sign for "All Trails." Take the path down to the Baker River—here a large brook. Turn left, then in a few yards, turn right over the foot-bridge. On the west bank, the Gorge Brook Trail begins to your left. (To the right, the Asquam-Ridge Trail leads upstream for a much longer route to the summit via the Beaver Brook Trail.)

Take the path left along the bank. About opposite the Ravine Lodge, the trail swings right, and you begin the

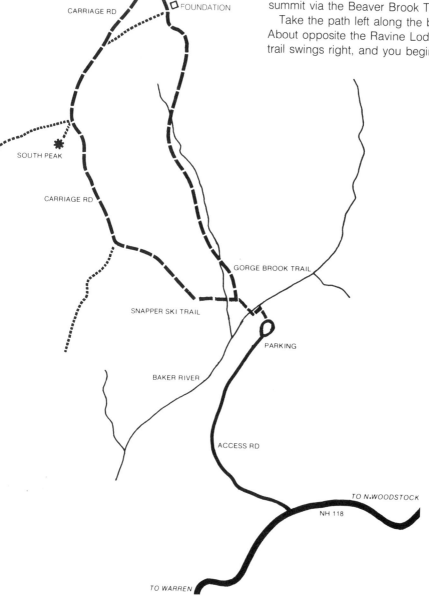

MT MOOSILAUKE

FOUNDATION

CARRIAGE RD

SOUTH PEAK

CARRIAGE RD

GORGE BROOK TRAIL

SNAPPER SKI TRAIL

PARKING

BAKER RIVER

ACCESS RD

TO N. WOODSTOCK

NH 118

TO WARREN

Rime ice

climb. After ¼ mile the Snapper Ski Trail branches left. (In combination with a section of the Carriage Road, it will be your return route—unless a storm hits the summit.) The Gorge Brook Trail is more direct, rising steadily toward the summit. It follows an old logging road through mixed growths of hardwoods and spruces beside Gorge Brook's pools and cascades. The trail crosses Gorge Brook twice before the steepest section about 1 mile from the start. A trail up Gorge Brook Slide diverges left to the Carriage Road. The main Gorge Brook Trail continues steeply upward through spruce/fir woods, home of the 3,000-foot bird, the blackpoll warbler.

Approaching treeline, the trail becomes more gradual, and the views begin to open up. Scrubby heaths alternate with twisted evergreens. You pass the cabin foundation on your right and a spring on your left. Don't drink the water. The trail, marked by cairns up the treeless alpine sward and ledges, continues northerly to the rocky summit, to the rectangular stone foundations that once supported the Summit House, and to the encompassing panorama.

To descend by the Snapper Ski Trail, take the Carriage Road south along the rocky ridge. If this is hidden in cloud, return to the cabin foundations and turn right, into the scrub on a section of the Appalachian Trail, which passes little mountain meadows and joins the Carriage Road where it is easier to follow in fog. (If a storm threatens while you are on the summit, return by the Gorge Brook Trail.) About 1 mile south of the summit on the Carriage Road, the Glencliff Trail, a link in the route the Appalachian Trail follows to Hanover and on into Vermont, drops down into the woods, right.

Just beyond the Glencliff Trail, a short spur leads west to the south peak for a view of the forested Baker River valley, Lake Tarleton, Mount Cube, Smarts Mountain, and various ponds.

Keep on the Carriage Road for 1 mile, passing the Gorge Brook Slide Trail on the left, and descending the rocky, washed-out track to the Snapper Ski Trail, where you turn left. This is now a footpath with views over steep drops. The loop is completed down at Gorge Brook Trail, about 1 mile.

Mount Garfield

Distance (round trip): 9¼ miles
Walking time: 5½ hours
Vertical rise: 3,100 feet
Maps: USGS 7½' Franconia; USGS 7½' South Twin Mt.

Mount Garfield's rocky summit commands a spectacular and unique view across a northern valley of the Pemigewasset "Wilderness." Due south from Mount Garfield, Owl's Head—itself a 4,023-foot Mountain—blocks the valley and forces Franconia Brook east, while forming a narrow gap below the Franconia Range. There, on the west, Mounts Lafayette and Lincoln rise to a heavy, peaked ridge. Mount Liberty stands alone, and Flume's spire farther south has its separate identity.

You look east down to AMC's Garfield Ridge Campsite and Shelter. Away off in that direction, Galehead Hut appears as a toy building among miles of evergreens. A line of summits shapes the eastern horizon and extends southward from North Twin over South Twin, Zealand Mountain, Guyot, and Bond to Bondcliff in the Pemigewasset River's East Branch valley.

The Garfield Trail approaches the mountain from US 3 and takes you up the long western slope to the steep cone, at 4,488 feet.

Drive north through Franconia Notch on US 3. At the I-93 junction, keep right, toward Twin Mountain, 5 miles. There's a wide turnout, right, before the bridge

over Gale River. Take the Forest Service road leaving the turnout left, and follow it 1.3 miles to the trail-head. For parking, turn left over a bridge above the Gale River's South Branch. Return to the trail and follow a logging road up the west bank. After ¼ mile the Garfield Trail turns left across the brook. (The logging road bears right.)

The trail leads up gradually, through fine woods to crossings at Thompson and Spruce Brooks. (Last sure water.) The good walking continues. This is one of the pleasantest trails in the mountains, but, for years after a forest fire in 1902, the trail traversed burned country. As often happens in logged and burned land, birches took over. Now their white trunks shine in sunlight along the trail. Farther removed on either side you sometimes look into the thickly sprouting clearcuts of the early 1970s.

After a short downhill grade below a ledgy bank, left, the trail climbs the steeper slope by long inclines between switchback turns. The birches yield to spruce/fir woods higher up. The trail steepens as it bears east. The evergreens become smaller, with gnarled birch and mountain ash interspersed beside the rocky outcrops and stone

View of Mt. Garfield

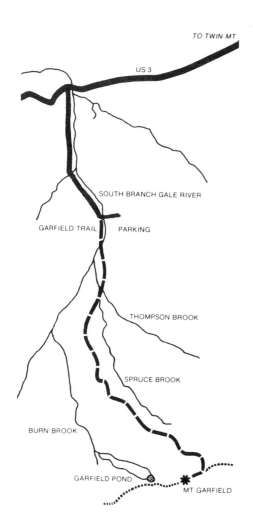

steps that now often form the trail.

Climbing around a corner to the right, you head south to join the Garfield Ridge Trail for the summit approach. (This trail comes up on the left from the Garfield Ridge Campsite.) The two trails ascend as one for a scramble of less than ¼ mile up the final pitch. The trail suggests a crude rock stairway between low spruces, which offer handholds.

At the crest, turn left. It's 50 yards to the summit rocks and a former tower's concrete foundation. (Garfield Ridge Trail continues to Mount Lafayette.)

In August 1907, Mount Garfield overlooked a holocaust. Twenty-five thousand acres, left in slash by J. E. Henry's logging, burst into flame as lightning struck the east side of Owl's Head. This fire was one of many that brought militant attention to the desolation caused by lumbermen, and led to the Weeks Bill of 1911 that established the White Mountain National Forest.

There's no loop to this hike. Return by the same route you came.

Mount Osceola

Distance (Tripoli Road to main peak and return):
  7 miles
Walking time: 4½ hours
Vertical rise: 2,025 feet
Maps: USGS 15′ Plymouth; USGS 7½′ Mt. Osceola

Tripoli Road, Breadtray Ridge, Thornton Gap, Scar Ridge, Mad River—these colorful names from loggers' parlance enliven maps of the country that surrounds this peak named for the famous Seminole warrior. Mount Osceola dominates the upper end of Waterville Valley. Its 4,326-foot elevation viewed from the west appears as a single summit, but, seen from the east along the Kancamagus Highway, the East Peak's 4,185-foot shoulder enlarges the mountain.

The most direct trail to the main summit begins at Waterville Valley's northwest pass, Thornton Gap. From Campton drive east on NH 49, 10 miles up the Mad River. Turn left, and drive past the access road to Tecumseh Ski Area. This Tripoli Road crests 4.5 miles from NH 49 at the 2,300-foot pass. About 200 yards

On Mt. Osceola

beyond, the Mount Osceola Trail enters the woods on the right (north). Park opposite along the roadside.

Through second-growth cherry and poplar trees, you climb an old tractor road to a stony section between young white birches. The trail becomes a series of gravel switchbacks. You look off to Mount Tripyramid's North Slide. More switchbacks take you up Breadtray Ridge to views of Mount Tecumseh's ski trails and Sandwich Mountain to the south beyond the green Waterville Valley. At a log-bridged gully, you stop at a spring, left, among spruces at the head of a little brook. Climbing again, you walk over log steps that prevent washouts, swing left more steeply, then right and left several times. Near the top of the ridge, the trail turns sharply right, east, and leads up to the level approach through summit spruces to the ledges and tower. The lowest stairs have been detached from the tower. Like various other unused towers in the White Mountain National Forest, it will probably be taken down.

You now stand on the highest of the mountains encircling Waterville Valley. Slightly south of east, Mount Tripyramid's three peaks notch the horizon five miles away. An unusual nearby view extends north into the valley along Hancock Branch and the Kancamagus Highway. On the right of Mount Hancock, and more distant, Mount Carrigain's angular bulk gives you a line on Mount Washington, twenty-two miles away. Turning northwest, you can orient yourself by the sentinel, Mount Garfield, and find to your left Mounts Lafayette and Lincoln. Of the remaining Franconias, Mounts Liberty and Flume are pinnacles in the direction of Cannon Mountain. More to the west, Kinsman's north and south summits appear as a ridge, but Mount Moosilauke stands out as the important western peak.

Return to Tripoli Road by the route of ascent.

Those hardy souls who yearn to climb all the accepted 4,000-foot peaks will continue east on the Mount Osceola Trail, and will think nothing of the descent and climb to East Peak 1 mile away. They may even keep on down the steep and hazardous trail to Greeley Ponds and out to the Kancamagus Highway for a total of 7 miles from the Tripoli Road. (See Hike 8.) This exploit requires 2 more hours than Osceola alone, and arrangement for transportation at the end.

Mount Tripyramid

Distance (round trip): 10½ miles
Walking time: 7 hours
Vertical rise (including all three peaks): 3,050 feet
Maps: USGS 15′ Plymouth; USGS 15′ Mt. Chocorua

The name describes the three peaks; it says nothing about the two slides. For pure joy in climbing, the North Slide is hard to beat. You choose your own way over the angular ledges. There is little danger in dry weather. A wild and extensive view opens behind you.

From the Livermore Road out of Waterville Valley, you hike a loop up the exciting North Slide, over the three peaks, down the treacherous South Slide, and back to the road. The slides tore out the woods and rocks on both North and South Peaks in 1885. The slides are completely unlike, the North Slide being ledges, the South Slide rocks and gravel. The three peaks rise in a line from a ridge about 1 mile long. North Peak's elevation is 4,140 feet. Middle Peak reaches to 4,110 feet. South Peak crests at 4,090 feet.

From Campton, drive east on NH 49, 10 miles up the Mad River. Turn left onto the Tripoli Road and drive past the access road to Tecumseh Ski Area. At 1.8 miles from NH 49, turn right across the Mad River's West Branch. Keep left at a fork just beyond the bridge. Unless logging operations interfere, you can drive .5 mile to park at a clearing known as Depot Camp. In this area extensive

cleanup logging was necessary after the gale of December 3, 1980, which devastated Waterville Valley. (There is also parking on the left, halfway to Depot Camp.)

From your car, walk to the east corner of the clearing and around a locked gate barring vehicles. Cross a small bridge. Your route is straight ahead along the Forest Service's Livermore Road. Keep past the Greeley Ponds Trail on your left. You soon cross a bridge over the Mad River.

The Livermore Road has been graded for trucks removing logs from clearcuts south of the road. As well as logging roads in that direction, you'll pass various trails that are part of the hiking and ski touring system maintained by the Waterville Valley Athletic and Improvement Association. At 1¾ miles from Depot Camp there's a main logging road to the right across Avalanche Brook on a creosoted, heavy-timbered bridge. Don't take it. Stay on your side of the brook, the north or left bank, and on the "unimproved" old Livermore Road.

Twenty minutes of this easy walking will bring you to the trail on the right for Tripyramid's South Slide. It is your return route after you climb over the mountain's

MIDDLE & SOUTH
TRI-PYRAMID
→
NORTH PEAK

SABBADAY BROOK TRAIL
← 3.9 SABBADAY FALLS
← 4.3 KANCAMAGUS HWY.

LBANY INTERVA

Trail signs on Mt. Tripyramid

three summits. Another half mile and you pass through the opening that was once Avalanche Camp back during the axe-crosscut-saw era in the White Mountains. You are approaching the start of the climb—it's half a mile farther for a total of 3¼ miles from Depot Camp. Watch for a hairpin turn to the left. The trail to the North Slide drops off the road to your right at the corner. (The Livermore Road continues and becomes a hiker's trail over Livermore Pass and down to the Kancamagus Highway four miles north.)

(Note: The Slide is dangerous when wet or icy. For a trail that bypasses it, proceed up the Livermore Road ¼ mile and turn right onto the Scaur Ridge Trail. This trail loops eastward toward Scaur Peak and a ridge connecting with North Tripyramid, where it joins the Pine Bend Brook Trail coming up from the Kancamagus Highway to the North Peak. This safer route is only about ¾ mile longer than via the North Slide.)

On a dry, warm day, climb down from the hairpin turn and cross Avalanche Brook. This is the last water until the base of South Slide. Climb the bank beyond the brook and take an old logging road upstream, left, for a half mile walk to the base of the slide. Yellow blazes on the rocks show you the route. If you wander off between pauses to turn and admire the view behind you, just remember to bear right near the top. The trail enters the spruces at the upper left corner of the west section, which is on your right.

The short remaining climb in the woods takes you to the North Peak and open ledges with a tremendous 180-degree view starting in the west and swinging northwest to include the Franconia Ridge and farther around to Mount Washington, northeast—all from a rare angle across the Kancamagus Highway and over the forests of the Pemigewasset "Wilderness".

To proceed on the trail from North Peak, face away from the view. Joining from the left, Pine Bend Brook Trail becomes the trail south down the ridge. It ends after ½ mile at the Sabbaday Brook Trail, left (from the Kancamagus Highway). You keep straight along and begin the climb up and over Middle Peak, then South Peak. Descending, you come to the South Slide and to forested vistas stretching away west. The two Flat Mountain Ponds lie in a hollow left of Sandwich Mountain. Ski trails identify Mount Tecumseh. Mount Moosilauke dominates the western horizon.

About halfway down the slide at a sign and cairn, the Sleeper Trail comes in on your left from Mount Whiteface. Keep on down the slide. Watch for rolling gravel and loose rocks as you place your feet. At the base of the slide, bear right. The trail enters the woods and runs above Slide Brook to a crossing over Avalanche Brook and the terminus at the Livermore Road. Turn left down the road for the return to your car.

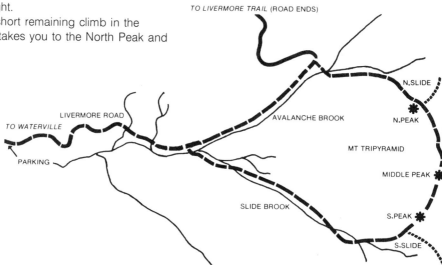

TO LIVERMORE TRAIL (ROAD ENDS)

LIVERMORE ROAD

TO WATERVILLE

PARKING

AVALANCHE BROOK

N.SLIDE

N.PEAK

MT TRIPYRAMID

MIDDLE PEAK

SLIDE BROOK

S.PEAK

S.SLIDE

31

Between the Notches: Zeacliff

Distance (round trip via Twinway): 7½ miles
  (round trip, including loop through Zealand Notch):
  9¼ miles
Walking time (via Twinway): 4½ hours
  (through Zealand Notch): 6½ hours
Vertical rise: 1,500 feet
Map: USGS 15′ Crawford Notch

The roadless upper watershed of the Pemigewasset River's East Branch separates Franconia Notch and Crawford Notch and their adjacent mountains. The main highways circle this country and leave the tourist unaware of the forested valleys and peaks between the two sections of the White Mountains. A hike to Zeacliff fills this vacancy.

You approach this great outlook along an abandoned railroad grade once used to haul logs out to the mills. The grade parallels the Zealand River toward its source. Beavers dam the branching streams. Zealand Pond, at the end of swampy meadows, has two outlets. Mid-June is a fine time to walk the Zealand Trail and look for birds. At that time, too, the rhodora blooms pink across the bogs.

Perched above the pond, AMC's Zealand Falls Hut offers accommodations to thirty-six hikers and a view directly to Mount Carrigain.

Zeacliff is about 1¼ miles above by the Twinway, a mountain trail. This steady climb brings you to Zeacliff's lookoff ledge above wooded valleys and mountains stretching away south and east, with views of Zealand Notch and Whitewall Mountain, both seared by fire during and after the logging days of the 1880s and early 1900s. This old, slashed and burned country has grown up largely to hardwoods. Former logging roads appear as green ribbons along distant contours of lighter growth. Sometimes ravens hover over the cliffs.

To reach the beginning of the Zealand Trail and the railroad grade, drive to Zealand Campground on US 302 2.5 miles east from Twin Mountain village. Turn south on the Forest Service's Zealand Road, which crosses the Ammonoosuc River and leads up a steep hill to a steadily ascending valley. Pass the Sugarloaf Camping Area and continue to the Zealand Road's end, 3.5 miles from the highway.

To reach the Zealand Trail, walk to the south end of the parking area. Continue past the gate at the bulletin board, over a bridge across Hoxie Brook, to the road's end 100 yards farther on. The Zealand Trail follows the railroad grade except for short sections cut through the woods where the railroad once crossed the Zealand River for short distances. In this way the trail keeps west of the dwindling river, which divides into its source streams. You approach Zealand Pond through a boggy country of

Near Zeacliff

meadows and beaver ponds.

At 2¼ miles from the start of the Zealand Trail, the A–Z Trail enters from the left. (The A–Z Trail connects to trails from the Crawford House site and Crawford Notch's Willey Range.) You cross the north outlet of Zealand Pond and follow the east shore. At the south end, where you make a sharp right turn, the Ethan Pond Trail enters from the left. (The Ethan Pond Trail leads through Zealand Notch.) Keep right, across a wet section at the south outlet of Zealand Pond. Soon you climb the trail's only steep rise to its terminus at the Zealand Falls Hut, 2,700 feet elevation.

Behind the hut, take the Twinway Trail up past the Lend-a-Hand Trail at the right. (The Lend-a-Hand Trail climbs Mount Hale.) Cross the small Whitewall Brook above the falls. Here is the last water. The Twinway Trail is rough and steep compared to the previous railroad grade. White birches grow smaller as the trail climbs into stunted spruces. It emerges on the rocky summit of the

ridge leading toward Zealand Mountain, Mount Guyot, and South Twin. At an unmarked fork in the trail just before the summit rocks, bear left for the top of

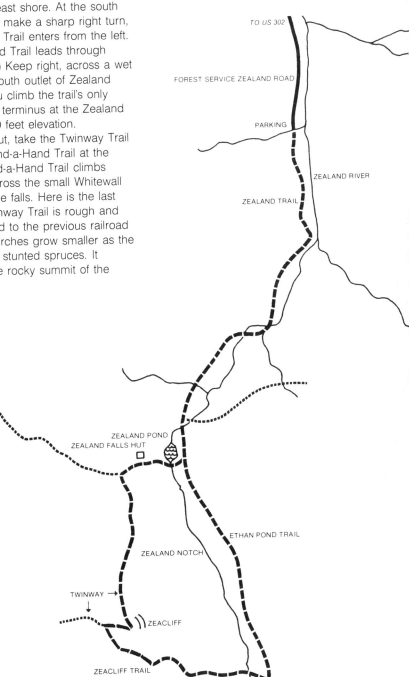

TO US 302

FOREST SERVICE ZEALAND ROAD

PARKING

ZEALAND RIVER

ZEALAND TRAIL

ZEALAND POND
ZEALAND FALLS HUT

ETHAN POND TRAIL

ZEALAND NOTCH

TWINWAY →

ZEACLIFF

ZEACLIFF TRAIL

Zeacliff, which is on a short loop off the main Twinway Trail. The cliff overlooks Zealand Notch and faces Whitewall Mountain.

You are looking across the Forest Service's Lincoln Woods Scenic Area, which consists of 18,560 acres preserved in their wildness. Mount Carrigain towers across the forest. Ponds draining into the Pemigewasset River's East Branch glisten in the valleys. To the left of Carrigain you sight through Carrigain Notch next to Mount Lowell. To the right of Carrigain, Mount Hancock is a solid outline. Closer and to the west, Mount Bond reaches away south from its barren crown.

If you are in shape for a tough and dramatic descent, your return need not be back to the hut the way you came. Fair warning: this loop is not for picnickers. If you decide you're rugged enough, walk west along the Twinway amost ¼ mile and turn left onto the Zeacliff Trail. It at once drops off the side of the mountain into evergreen forest with eroded roots, rocks, and bare rock faces sometimes more than ten feet high. You descend into a forest of white birches along a southerly ridge, then drop again in a series of steep pitches between level little plateaus. Through the leaves you may catch glimpses of the slides and cliffs of Whitewalll Mountain across Zealand Notch.

You reach the bottom of the ridge at a stretch of spruce and balsam woods before you come to the alders along Whitewall Brook. It's a tidy little stream, and you can cross on rocks, usually. Beyond it you climb a wooded slide into the open of barren rock slabs and jagged talus. The formations suggest an abandoned quarry. Follow blue blazes up this rock-scramble to the Ethan Pond Trail. Turn left, north, for the hike back to Zealand Pond along the old railroad grade. This loop is a distance of 3 miles as compared to the 1¼ miles back the way you came from Zealand Falls Hut. But it's an experience passing through Zealand Notch before hiking out to your car.

Mount Washington
Region

Pinkham Notch: The Crew-Cut Trail

Distance (round trip): 1¾ miles
Walking time: 1¼ hours
Vertical rise: 400 feet
Maps: USGS 15' Mt. Washington; USGS 7½' Carter Dome

Pinkham Notch appears less spectacular near the highway than either Franconia or Crawford Notch. But, situated close under Mount Washington's eastern ravines, Pinkham Notch has its own distinction: it's a climbing center. It's as near as you can drive on a main highway (NH 16) to the most impressive mountain in New England—Mount Washington. Major trails pass through or start in Pinkham Notch. It's the mountain climbers' base, a takeoff for the Presidential Range.

Pinkham Notch has changed since 1826, when Daniel Pinkham built the road through his grant between Jackson and Randolph. Now there's the wide highway: traffic on NH 16 would astound Daniel Pinkham. The AMC Pinkham Notch Camp (10 miles north of Jackson), established in 1920, has outgrown the original log cabins and has become a complex, modern headquarters for the

AMC Huts and Trail System, with plentiful parking and accommodations for a hundred guests. At Wildcat Ski Area the gondola lift operates year round.

As part of an introductory hike, the 1-mile Crew-Cut Trail winds through hardwood forest to a lookout ledge at the north end of Pinkham Notch. To start the hike, turn west off NH 16 at Pinkham Notch Camp. Park along the old road. Walk past the lodge toward Mount Washington. Turn right to the Tuckerman

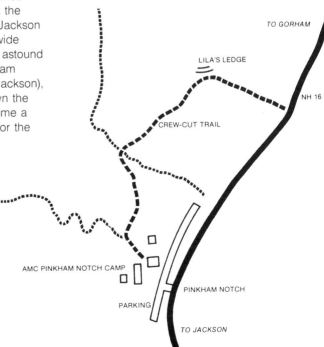

Ravine Trail. About 300 feet past the buildings on the right, watch for the sign to the Old Jackson Road. Bear right on this trail. Cross a work road, following the yellow disks on trees. The trail winds through open woods ¼ mile to a junction where the unused section of the Old Jackson Road comes in from the highway. A few yards to the left along the road, the Crew-Cut Trail branches right. Follow the red paint blazes across a seasonal brook and swing left. After a short distance, the trail makes a right turn.

The trail requires attention if it is to be followed through this section among beech and yellow birch trees. Across the second brook, keep straight past the George's Gorge Trail, left. Orange paint blazes supplement the older red blazes.

The trail climbs over a knoll and enters an area of broken ledges under the tall trees as it approaches the base of a cliff. The main trail turns sharply right. A spur trail leads straight to the lookout called Lila's Ledge. This pinnacle offers a view from its lower corner toward Wildcat Ski Area. Above, for the experienced and agile climber, a wide view opens into Pinkham Notch and up to Mount Washington.

The main trail, avoiding the cliff, curves left and goes down steeply across several levels of the slope. It passes through the seepage from a small bog shortly before reaching NH 16, fifty yards south and opposite the ski area's parking lot.

Return to your car by the same route you came.

33

Lowe's Bald Spot

Distance (round trip): 4¼ miles
Walking time: 2¾ hours
Vertical rise: 1,000 feet
Map: USGS 15′ Mt. Washington

Treeline warning sign, Mt. Washington

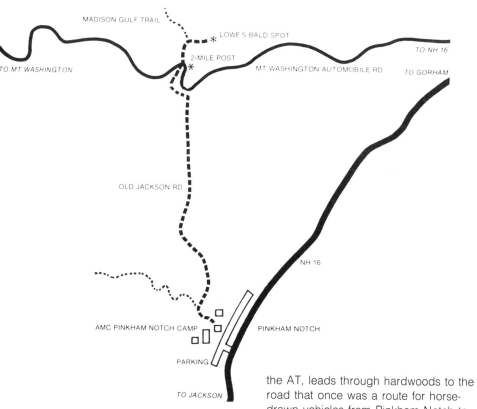

The half-day excursion from Pinkham Notch to Lowe's Bald Spot takes you to a 3,000-foot opening on Mount Washington's eastern slope. By easy trails you experience the mountain's sweep and primitive power. You look away to the peaks north and west. Wide views open east to the Carter Range and south through Pinkham Notch. Lowe's Bald Spot gives you mountain air and sunlight, distant skies and the near scent of fir balsam. You may even forget asphalt highways, cars, cities, and mortgage payments.

Turn off NH 16 for parking at the AMC Pinkham Notch Camp. Beyond the lodge take the Tuckerman Ravine Trail for 50 yards to the branch trail right, leading to the Old Jackson Road. The trail, part of the AT, leads through hardwoods to the road that once was a route for horse-drawn vehicles from Pinkham Notch to the carriage road, now the auto road. It rises about 600 feet in the 1¼ miles before you leave it at a sharp left turn onto a 1977 trail cut to avoid a section of the auto road (once part of this hike).

The bypass trail rises steeply for a few yards before leveling somewhat and passing the Raymond Path to your left, then the Nelson Crag Trail, also left. (See Hike 37, The Alpine Garden on Mount Washington.) Keep on past these junctions and climb to a gravel pit, which the trail crosses. You come out on the auto road above the two-mile marker. On the other side of the road, take the Madison Gulf Trail. You are continuing on the AT as it enters the Great Gulf Wilderness. (No permit required for day hikes, but for overnight use during the snow-free season you must have a free Wilderness Permit. See the introduction.)

Follow the Madison Gulf Trail ¼ mile to a branch trail, right, and the short climb to Lowe's Bald Spot. (The Madison Gulf Trail continues to the Great Gulf, up to treeline, and to the AMC Madison Hut in the barren col between Mount Adams and Mount Madison, the northeastern pinnacle of the Presidential Range. The Trail is also a link to the Great Gulf Trail and the trails leaving the Gulf for the high peaks. The entire Madison Gulf Trail takes five hours of steady hiking and strenuous climbing up the steep headwall of Madison Gulf.)

After the short climb from the main trail to Lowe's Bald Spot, you look north across the lower valley of the Great Gulf and the West Branch of the Peabody River to Mount Adams and Mount Madison. West is the headwall of Huntington Ravine topped by Nelson Crag and the bare cone of Mount Washington, a desert of jumbled stones rising in unforgettable contrast to the green trees below. Up there, earth's verdure emerges miraculously from its mineral source. Yet the grim environment might suggest to you an atomic blast's rubble. If it does, you are happy to hear the birds singing in the nearby spruces and to see hikers on the trails, and almost relieved to hear autos grinding up the road.

Glen Boulder

Distance (to Glen Boulder and back): 3 miles
Walking time: 3 hours
Vertical rise: 1,800 feet
Map: USGS 15′ Crawford Notch

West of the highway (NH 16) through Pinkham Notch and about eight miles north of Jackson, a high bare ridge supports Glen Boulder among lesser rocks. Outlined against the sky, the great boulder appears about to topple into the Notch.

A climb to this landmark also lifts you rapidly to treeline with its strange ecology of ledge and lichen. Glen Boulder is a good destination for an afternoon. Besides being the shortest route to treeline on this eastern side of Mount Washington, it tests your legs and offers a superb panorama of mountainous slopes, valleys, and summits

The Glen Boulder Trail, cut and marked in 1905, leaves the parking circle and rest rooms at Glen Ellis Falls on the west side of NH 16, 9 miles north of Jackson. (Glen Ellis Falls, reached by a tunnel under the highway and by stone steps into a ravine, sluices spectacularly from a ledge seventy feet into a rocky pool. The water of Ellis River pours out as from a pitcher. Mist cools the air blowing across the evergreens and the pool, where sightseers click cameras.)

The Glen Boulder Trail, rising from the parking area's south corner, slabs across a steep service road and swings right,

climbing to level woods. Here you pass through a typical 2,000-foot elevation hardwood forest. Big yellow birches, beeches, and other deciduous trees shade striped maples, hobble bushes, and ferns. Wood thrushes and hermit thrushes inhabit the ground and undergrowth.

At the second steep pitch, which takes you to the base of a cliff, the trail divides. To the left the Chimney Route offers a rugged scramble up a gully and ledges. To the right the Chimney Bypass is the easier route, although steep. I advise choosing it. Just above the cliff the trail takes you to the junction, on your right, with the Direttissima, a trail leading in one mile to Pinkham Notch Camp.

Climbing on, as the Glen Boulder Trail and its orange blazes swing left, you pass after five minutes the Chimney Route coming in on your left. Beyond this, a spur trail, left, leads to a view up the Notch and across to Wildcat Mountain. The main trail soon begins a steep ascent. Ten minutes above the junction of the Chimney Route, you cross a ski touring trail marked with blue squares. After one-half hour of steady climbing, you cross a brook and approach the abruptly rising shoulder. From here you

Glen Boulder

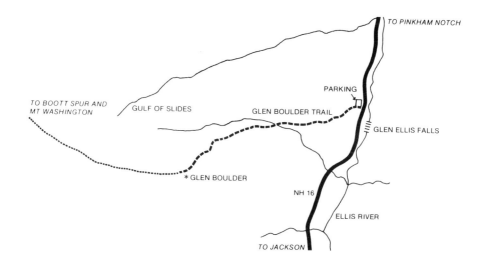

climb from treeline through alpine vegetation, wind-and-snow-flattened black spruce/balsam — known as krummholz — over steep ledges and rocks, for ¼ mile up to Glen Boulder.

Facing south you look away twenty miles to Mount Chocorua's rocky tower. The sweep is to your left over the Saco River and Ellis River valleys to nearby Wildcat Ridge and around over Pinkham Notch to Mount Washington.

The Glen Boulder Trail continues steeply above treeline and through scrub spruce for more than one and one-half miles to the Davis Path. This fine route to Mount Washington should be undertaken only by seasoned climbers. From Glen Boulder to Mount Washington's summit via the Davis Path and the Crawford Path is a rugged, long four miles. A loop to the AMC Lakes-of-the-Clouds Hut adds another one mile. These trails are more difficult than they appear and take longer than you might estimate; allow three hours of constant walking and climbing, at least, even in good weather. If there's any sign of clouds descending, rain, or storm, turn around at the boulder and descend to your car.

This is also a warning to the beginner and to the exhilarated devotee who feels a powerful urge to go on just a while longer. You planned a short climb to Glen Boulder. Enjoy yourself there, then head back.

And don't take the Direttissima, or you'll end up at Pinkham Notch Camp. Keep to the right of that junction.

Tuckerman Ravine

Distance (to the Snow Arch and back): 6¼ miles
Walking time: 5 hours
Vertical rise: 2,300 feet
Map: USGS 15′ Mt. Washington

A glacial cirque of rocks and cliffs gouged at treeline by prehistoric ice, this dramatic basin in Mount Washington's southeast slope can be an exciting destination as well as the beginning of the strenuous upper climbing to the summit. Open-front shelters amid spruces surround little Hermit Lake. The headwall's precipices are famous for spring skiing when they are banked by tremendous snow accumulations; they drip veils of water that gather at the base to undercut the remaining snow and form the Snow Arch, which survives well into summer.

On the north, the cliff named Lion Head juts into the Ravine toward the south wall, which is crowned by Boott Spur. East, from the open half-basin, the view extends across Pinkham Notch to Wildcat Ridge and the Carter Range. Climbing directly from the Notch into this giant amphitheater, the Tuckerman Ravine Trail follows a graded tractor path 2½ miles up to Hermit Lake and the shelters.

Drive north from Jackson on NH 16 for 10 miles until you come to a large sign on the west side identifying the AMC Pinkham Notch Camp. Turn in and leave your car in the long parking strip, where other hikers, young and old, are preparing to leave for the trails or are returning. Here at the AMC lodge you'll find information on the trails, a snack bar, and other facilities. (Here also you may obtain the permit required if you plan to stay overnight in the Ravine's shelters.)

To reach the Tuckerman Ravine Trail, walk past the main lodge and turn right. Keep to the wide tractor path. It presents good footing and equable grades suitable for all hikers regardless of experience or ability; but it's still an uphill climb and hikers intending to climb above treeline should take to heart the warning sign about adequate clothing and food and good physical condition.

The path crosses Cutler River, named soon after the Revolution for an explorer, the Reverend Manasseh Cutler. His party changed the mountain's name from Agiochook to Washington. Beyond the footbridge over this stream whose source is far up under the headwall, you turn a right corner and begin to climb. Soon, on the right again, take a few steps up to a ledge across from Crystal Cascade, one of the most impressive in the mountains.

The path continues to climb by easy switchbacks through a forest of big yellow birch and beech. These woods

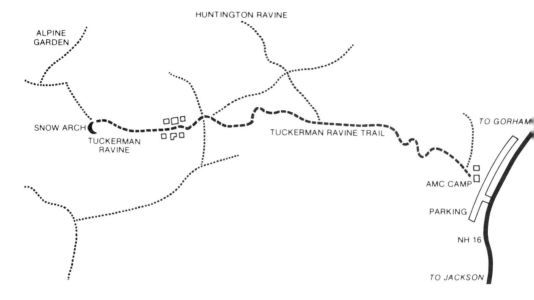

are favored by the winter wren, in summer only, despite his name. He's notable for his small size and for his vertical tailfeathers. You hear his voluble song more often than you see him in the underbrush.

After about 1 mile, the woods change to spruce and fir interspersed with white birch and mountain ash. You may expect to catch glimpses of boreal chickadees in the evergreens. Their brown caps differentiate them from the common black-capped chickadees. The boreals sing a husky series of notes lacking one or two "dees." Rare until the last few years, they seem to have discovered and taken over the cool White Mountains, which lie south of their regular habitat.

Along the Tuckerman Ravine Trail, access links to the John Sherburne Ski Trail occur at intervals on the left. These are marked by signs and can be easily avoided. Stay on the graded tractor path. Continue past the Huntington Ravine Trail, which branches right. Cross a wooden bridge over the Cutler River, where hikers often rest and admire the view toward Wildcat Ridge.

Two miles of steady climbing take you past the Raymond Path on the right and around a wide S-turn into the Ravine. You pass the Lion Head Trail, right, and the Boott Spur Link on the left. The Ravine opens up to the wide sky and bare rocks. The shelters appear along side trails and across Hermit Lake.

The central building, once known as "Howard Johnson's," burned in 1972, but has been rebuilt and serves as an information center and caretaker's lodge. No meals are available. The old name, applied satirically years ago to an earlier building that also burned, expressed the attitude of various salty characters who preferred the primitive Ravine when it had only two log shelters. Cliffs tower above, and, to the west, beyond a rocky slope edged with scrub spruce, the headwall rises perpendicularly toward clouds that coast steadily eastward.

The open-front shelters are for the eighty-six overnight hikers who obtain permits at the Pinkham Notch Camp. There is a small fee. Overuse of the

Tuckerman Ravine Headwall

limited area, as throughout the mountains at certain popular spots, has made new regulations necessary. Camping in the woods has been discontinued to preserve the delicate subalpine soil, trees, and plant life. Hikers should bring their own lunches and carry out their own trash. If cooking is planned, they should carry portable stoves; wood or charcoal fires are not allowed. The endangered ecology is responding to these conservation measures; hikers realize the problem and help.

A ¾-mile climb over a trail now rough and rocky leads you to the headwall and the Snow Arch. (This is still Tuckerman Ravine Trail continuing from the shelter areas on the north or right side of the brook.) Never walk under the Snow Arch. Huge chunks fall off without warning. By late summer it has melted away into Cutler River.

The Tuckerman Ravine Trail finds a route over rocks at the base of the cliffs, and circles the headwall to the north of the cliffs. Hikers on holiday weekends form a moving line of figures on the trail up and across the headwall. Balmy weather in the Ravine sometimes changes to icy wind and clouds above; plan on its doing so.

The summit of Mount Washington is only 1 mile from the Snow Arch, but it's a mile to remember. Time is a better measure: two hours, if you are accustomed to scrambling over rocks at such an angle. The 1,000 feet up to the summit from the diverging trails above the headwall (known as Tuckerman Junction) appear less because above treeline there is no familiar sight for estimating distance. The landscape is as strange as the sudden storms are fierce. And the higher you climb the fiercer they get; the protection of the Ravine is often welcome.

Mount Washington

Distance (round trip): 8 miles
Walking time: 8 hours
Vertical rise: 3,600 feet
Map: USGS 15′ Mt. Washington

By its western approach, the route of this climb to Mount Washington takes you up the steep and scenic Ammonoosuc Ravine from the cog railway's Base Station. Just above treeline, the AMC Lakes-of-the-Clouds Hut offers shelter if the weather turns frigid and stormy. Mount Washington's rocky cone and the summit buildings tower 1,200 feet higher and 1½ miles away at the top of the 165-year-old trail laid out by the legendary mountaineer, Ethan Allen Crawford.

On the summit, you'll meet tourists who came on the cog railway or in their cars. They think you are out of your mind for climbing when you could ride. For the dyed-in-the-wool hiker once or twice on the summit is enough, unforgettable as it is.

Save this climb for a day of matchless clarity, so rare on this peak of cloud, rain, and storm. Waiting for a clear day will prove worthwhile. Then the far horizon will be the limit of vision, and you'll see a great sweep of country that includes most of New Hampshire and parts of Maine, Vermont, and the Province of Quebec. You will stand at the center of a circle two hundred miles in diameter, enclosing hundreds of mountains and valleys in thirty thousand square miles. Perhaps you'll see the ocean to the east, blending with the sky.

Leave US 302 at Fabyan and drive on the Base Road 7.5 miles to the cog railway's Base Station. At the bottom of the final hill before the parking area for passengers, turn right into the hikers' parking space. In the summer season an attendant collects the nominal fee and issues a car tag. Shoulder your pack. It should contain a heavy sweater, thick wool shirt, or insulated jacket, also a parka, a warm cap, and gloves. Rain gear is good insurance. Your lunch and water should be supplemented by emergency food for two meals. If you climb in shorts, carry warm pants. You are heading for an arctic-alpine zone.

Those barren heights appear above you as you walk up the road to the station. Nearby, gala-clad vacationers watch engineers in overalls, grimy firemen, and brakemen, or they visit the gift shop and snack bar while they await train time. Engines with tilted boilers puff smoke and steam from coal fires and push passenger cars up the steep track by means of a drive gear engaging the steel pins set between the two walls of a center rail. This was the invention of New Hampshire-born Sylvester Marsh. In 1869

President Ulysses S. Grant rode up the mountain on the first train, along with P. T. Barnum, who allowed that the next morning's sunrise was the "second greatest show on earth." (No overnight accommodations now.)

The Ammonoosuc Ravine Trail starts behind cabins on a knoll to the south of the station. It leads you through woods as you follow the small Ammonoosuc River on your left for 1½ miles to a fine waterfall and pool.

Across the stream you begin the precipitous ascent up steps among spruces. The trail faces you like a rough, rocky wall of earth reinforced with tree roots. Part way up this first steep section, a small sign and a spur trail on the right offer you the opportunity to see the brook's glittering torrent pour down a long stone sluice formed by ledges. Climbing on up the main trail, you pass wide carpets of green-leaved wood sorrel, which blooms white in mid-July. You come to another high falls where at this altitude the mountain or alpine avens bloom yellow in early July. Among open rocks, Labrador tea puts out white frilly flowers, and bog laurel shows pink blooms above moist turf.

Ten minutes climbing brings you to another falls and brook crossing, then soon to another. The spruces dwindle to the ancient dwarf clumps twisted and flattened by winds at treeline. The scrub growth ends at the vast expanse of rocks, which extends to Mount Washington's summit on your left. Follow cairns and yellow paint arrows the last 100 yards over the ledges to the Lakes-of-the-Clouds Hut on the windswept col between Mount Washington and Mount Monroe on your right.

This AMC hut is the largest (excluding the headquarters at Pinkham Notch Camp) in the nine-hut system. Stone walls first withstood the gales at 5,000 feet in 1915. Now expanded and modernized with a capacity of ninety guests, the hut is a popular stopover. Many hikers cross from the Tuckerman Ravine Trail, descend from Mount Washington, or traverse the seven-mile ridge from Crawford Notch. The hut is the terminus of the Ammonoosuc Ravine Trail.

Here the wind, and often clouds in the form of dense fog, as well as violent summer storms of rain, lightning, and sleet, decide for you whether or not you climb on toward the summit on this try. You will probably understand why unwary hikers above treeline on Mount Washington have perished from exposure in summer.

When the weather's favorable, take the Crawford Path from the hut and follow it between the two little lakes whose stony shores and ledges support alpine plants, sedges, and shrubs. These botanical miracles possess the unbelievable tenacity of mountain flora as long as nature's delicate balance remains undisturbed. Varieties of heaths such as alpine bilberry and mountain cranberry survive doggedly in niches of scant earth.

Beyond the second lake, on rising ground, the Camel Trail branches right to Boott Spur, and the Tuckerman Crossover leads to Tuckerman Junction above the Ravine. Keep on the Crawford Path. It is well worn. It is marked by cairns, each topped with a yellow-painted rock. The gradual climb here is straight toward Washington's summit. The Davis Path joins from the right as you near the actual ascent of the cone. Not far beyond, the Westside Trail splits left to circle the cone for climbers heading toward the northern peaks of the Presidential Range—Clay, Jefferson, Adams, and Madison. Watch for this fork and be sure to bear right; although the cairn markers are the same, there's no chance of confusion in clear weather.

Mount Washington's summit beckons ½ mile ahead. You pass patches of tough Bigelow sedge, which thrives in this exposed situation. Juncos also appear at home. Now you go up the cone in a passage among rocks. You climb the final shoulder and look away to the northern peaks. The Gulfside Trail comes in left from these peaks. You approach the summit from the north up the last rock slope.

Your introduction to the modern age on the summit can be jarring—television towers, transmitter buildings, two monster cylinders rising like rocket launchers, a railroad with steam engine and passenger car, the occupants from the train and tourists from the auto road wandering around, the old stone-walled Tip Top House still preserved for its

history—all appear insignificant compared to the extensive Sherman Adams Building partially encircling the actual summit. You are in the fifty-nine acre Mount Washington State Park. The top of the world in northeastern America is a ledge behind the Sherman Adams Building, 6,288 feet above sea level.

Inside the commodious building you'll find shelter from the wind, and wide views through the windows that curve around the lobby-dining room. You can visit the cafeteria, gift shop, museum, and information desk. The Mount Washington Observatory, a weather station, is also housed under the roof of concrete slabs.

If you are lucky enough to reach the

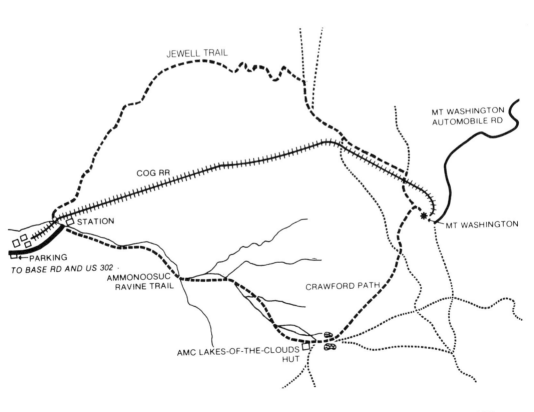

Mt. Washington, from Mt. Jefferson

summit early on a perfectly clear day and are fit for the challenge of more above-treeline balancing on rocks, you may want to descend by the Gulfside Trail and the Jewell Trail, as a loop back to the Base Station. Or you may *climb* by the Jewell Trail. It starts from across the tracks and a bridge over the Ammonoosuc River. The Gulfside Trail, which in sections could almost be described as paved with stones, takes you past the headwall of the awesome Great Gulf, the largest glacial cirque on Mount Washington. The Jewell Trail joins the Gulfside at the west slope of Mount Clay. Unlike the Gulfside, the Jewell Trail's upper section is composed of rugged slabs marked in yellow paint and by cairns when you are on the easier section above the evergreen scrub. The trail below treeline is a graded way, but don't attempt this trail in bad weather. The views are too magnificent to miss, and caution should guide your mountaineering on dangerous old Mt. Washington.

Unless you choose the Gulfside-Jewell variation, descend as you came up by the Crawford Path and Ammonoosuc Ravine Trail.

37

The Alpine Garden

Distance (round trip): 8½ miles
Walking time: 6½ hours
Vertical rise: 3,500 feet
Map: USGS 15′ Mt. Washington

The object of the climb to Mount Washington's Alpine Garden is enjoyment of the mountain rather than its conquest. This loop climb, with the Garden as its destination, is a rugged and demanding rock-scramble above tree line. But it's spectacular and shows you why the mountain is unique. The alpine-arctic environment at the Garden affords more attractions than the tourist mecca on the summit. In three hours you climb from the temperate zone to an arctic waste.

Yet despite its barren appearance, this mile-high "garden" displays many of the 110 plant species that live above treeline on Mount Washington and other Presidential peaks. Of this total, 75 are never found below these altitudes in New Hampshire. Most of the alpine plants occur at lower elevations in Alaska, northern Canada, Greenland, and arctic Eurasia.

The flower time, mid-June to July brings the Alpine Garden a miraculous shower of colors. Then you see yellow alpine avens, white diapensia, purple Lapland rosebay, and pink bilberry. The grasses, such as Bigelow sedge and three-forked rush, sprout new green blades.

The Alpine Garden's plateau interrupts Mount Washington's steep eastern slope. A curving, mile-long shelf between Tuckerman Ravine and Huntington Ravine, the Garden begins and ends above these tremendous gorges. You look into dizzying depths and contrast them with the spaciousness of the sweeping views across Pinkham Notch to the Carter and Wildcat ranges.

The climb to this elemental world begins at the AMC Pinkham Notch Camp 10 miles north of Jackson on NH 16. Park on the old road west of the present NH 16.

Walk past the lodge and turn right onto the Tuckerman Ravine Trail. (See Hike 32.) Follow this path for about 300 feet and watch on your right for the trail to the Old Jackson Road. It leads through open woods to a junction where the unused section of the Old Jackson Road comes in from the highway. This ancient wagon road, now a trail and part of the AT marked as usual with the white blazes, takes you past two local trail walks branching to your right and crosses a brook or two before ascending to a sharp left turn off the old grade onto a trail cut in 1977. (This avoids any climbing on the auto road, which was formerly required from the junction with the

Alpine flowers

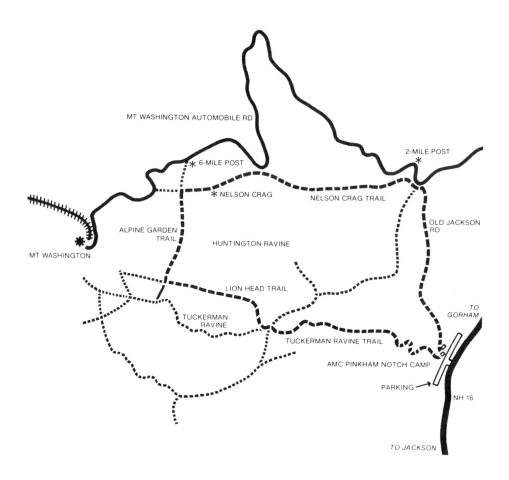

Old Jackson Road to the Nelson Crag Trail and others.)

The bypass trail rises steeply for a short distance. Then you pass the Raymond Path on your left—it leads to the Tuckerman Ravine Trail. Next you come to the Nelson Crag Trail. Turn left onto it. (For more information about the trail ahead and beyond the auto road see Hike 33: Lowe's Bald Spot.)

The Nelson Crag Trail heads west and almost at once goes directly at the mountain. This steep section leads you for a mile through evergreens, which become scrub at an open ridge with views of Pinkham Notch. Turning north over rocks, it joins the auto road above the 5-mile marker, and returns, left, to the rugged rocks on the side of Nelson Crag, which is not a single rock but a pile of huge rock slabs. A large cairn tells you that you've mastered the climb. Beyond the cairn you come to the Alpine Garden Trail between the auto road and Tuckerman Ravine. You are nearly a mile above sea level. (The Nelson Crag Trail continues between two rock-strewn knolls and joins the auto road again about six and one-half miles up from NH 16.)

At this junction take a good look at the weather. If you have any inkling that it will deteriorate in the next few hours or even if you are encountering ordinary clouds that are common above treeline, there is no point in continuing. The Alpine Garden is a gloomy rock field in cloud, and the cloud may be a warning of the deadly storms that blast Mount Washington. To retreat, turn right (north) on the Alpine Garden Trail and follow it to the auto road. Follow the auto road down to the Old Jackson Road for the return to Pinkham Notch Camp.

But, of course, if you've picked a clear day for this climb, the skies are blue and the sun is dazzling. In that happy event, turn left (south) from the Nelson Crag Trail onto the Alpine Garden Trail.

Soon you descend over rocks with views of Huntington Ravine on your left and the cone of Mount Washington on your right. A great cairn marks the junction with the Huntington Ravine Trail. Keep straight across. (The Huntington Ravine Trail climbs right one-quarter mile to the auto road. To your left, it descends over the dangerous rocks in the Ravine.) Now you are in the Alpine Garden, and ahead stretches the mile of scattered, broken stones among which grow the dwarf spruces, alpine plants, and shrubs. A pause for lunch gives you time to look about and absorb both the desolation and the life on this plateau, where plants not only survive but blossom in colors to match the rainbow.

(Warning note: Don't pluck or disturb the plants; they're unique, and they're protected. Don't drink from the little brook that crosses the Alpine Garden; it's contaminated by drainage from the summit.)

As you proceed, keep to the Alpine Garden Trail. Follow the cairns. The trail's worn rocks and tracked soil will guide you if a cloud descends—but pay attention. You cross a broad flat as you approach Tuckerman Ravine and the intersection with the Lion Head Trail. (The Alpine Garden Trail continues another one-quarter mile to the Tuckerman Ravine Trail.)

Turn left on the Lion Head Trail for magnificent views along the rim of Tuckerman Ravine. In June you will probably gaze down at skiers on late snow in the Ravine. The trail leads you over Lion Head's granite brow to a descent of its bare eastern shoulder. You step down from reinforcing logs at frequent intervals as the trail curves to your right into evergreen scrub and the lower spruce/fir woods. At the junction with the Tuckerman Ravine Trail, turn left. The trail is a tractor road here, which takes you down to Pinkham Notch Camp, 2¼ miles of easy walking.

Mount Jefferson

Distance (round trip): 6½ miles
Walking time: 6 hours
Vertical rise: 2,700 feet
Map: USGS 15' Mt. Washington

The sensational view south from Mount Jefferson's summit owes its fame to a vast glacial cirque, the Great Gulf, backed by the towering crags of Mount Washington. A remote peak of the Presidential Range if approached from the north, south, or east, and the third highest at 5,715 feet, Jefferson conceals its western access under the spruces that grow in Jefferson Notch. There the Caps Ridge Trail leaves the road and surmounts a sharp, west spur for the 2½-mile climb to the summit. Caps Ridge, however, should be approached warily rather than with the assurance that you've found the mountain's weak spot. The Caps Ridge Trail ascends the equivalent of a vertical ½ mile. There's no water.

The ledges, or Caps, challenge your legs and lungs. And the Caps present treacherous footing during or after a rainstorm.

From Mount Jefferson's summit, another spectacular shoulder, Castellated Ridge, provides a descent down the scenic Castle Trail, and a return route via the wooded Link Trail back to Caps Ridge Trail and Jefferson Notch. About 3 miles of this 6½-mile loop are above treeline.

To reach Jefferson Notch, turn off US 302 at Fabyan and follow the road toward the cog railway's Base Station. Drive about 5 miles to an intersection. Turn left there onto the Jefferson Notch Road (gravel). Careful driving and occasional use of low gear take you 3 miles up to 3,000 feet. You are in Jefferson Notch. Park on the right or left off the road.

The Caps Ridge Trail leads east through green spruce/fir woods. Leaving behind this wet and rooty section, you begin the real climb. Soon you catch glimpses of Mount Clay on the right.

The view opens at a smooth ledge, right, in which small potholes indicate glacial action. Continue up about ¼ mile and pass the Link Trail on the left. (Take note of this junction. You'll return along the Link on the loop from the summit.)

The evergreens become smaller as the trail rises steeply among jumbled rocks. You clamber up to treeline below the first of two jagged ledges called the Caps. About ¼ mile above, as the ridge becomes a sawtooth edge, you climb the second Cap. You are exposed to all the mountains and the sky. You're also exposed to the weather. If you see signs of rain, fog, or high winds, turn back while you can.

Climbing on under clear skies, you

Mt. Jefferson

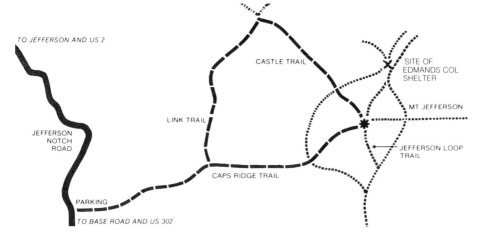

descend from the last Cap and start up the broad main peak. You cross the Cornice Trail, which for a few yards joins your Caps Ridge Trail. (The Cornice Trail, avoiding Jefferson's summit, offers a rough route left, north, to Edmands Col. To the right it swings southeast and joins the Gulfside Trail.) Here on the mountainside, open to the most violent and frigid winds, grass-like sedges and rushes thrive in little slanting meadows among acres of broken rock. In the fall—August at this altitude—these green swaths change to soft, pale tan colors.

Above the Cornice intersection, you may guess the next rise to be the summit, but you climb over two more before the cairns lead slightly left up the summit crags. Now you discover that Jefferson's summit consists of three crests bordering a lower flat, where signs mark the trail junction.

Each crest gives you an interesting perspective across the Great Gulf toward Mount Washington, its auto road, and summit buildings. The southeast ledges overlook Gulfside Trail's yellow-topped cairns crossing above the two ridges known as Jefferson's Knees. Looking east across Edmands Col to Mount Adams, you notice that it hides the last peak in the range, Mount Madison. (Note: the emergency shelter at Edmands Col east of Mount Jefferson on the Gulfside Trail has been removed.)

Your return loop begins at the junction between Jefferson's crests—in the hollow just east of the main summit—where you turn north onto Castle Trail. On Castle Trail cairns mark the way between the summit, left, and a rise of broken ledges, right. Swinging more northwest, you leave the small flat and descend toward distant rocks called the Castles. You follow a line of cairns easily spotted by their white quartz tops. The Castle Trail crosses the Cornice Trail. Less easily followed here, the cairns keep you seeking and picking your way down the scattered rock slabs toward the Castles. These vertical pinnacles overlook Castle Ravine's green depths. The trail becomes rougher and more difficult. It winds generally below, but sometimes over, the western crags along the narrow ridge.

After the ledges beyond the largest Castle, you descend steeply below treeline. The intersection with the Link Trail comes ten minutes later.

Turn left on the Link. (The Castle Trail continues down the ridge to Bowman on US 2.) For the first mile, the link crosses rough terrain over roots and rocks. Beyond a brook and during the second mile, the trail improves as it descends gradually through evergreen woods to an abrupt left turn up a few steep yards to the Caps Ridge Trail. There you turn right for Jefferson Notch and your car.

39

Mount Adams

Distance (round trip): 9 miles
Walking time: 7½ hours
Vertical rise: 4,500 feet
Map: USGS 15' Mt. Washington

Mount Adams fascinates and challenges many hikers more than any peak in the Presidential Range. It offers deep ravines and long ridges. Majestic views across the Great Gulf toward Mount Washington greet you from the summit crags. Mounts Jefferson and Madison seem like neighbors. Second in height to Washington at 5,798 feet, Mount Adams when climbed from the north demands 231 more vertical feet than Mount Washington from Pinkham Notch. This ruggedness guarantees no tourists.

The shortest trail up Mount Adams begins at Appalachia, a former railroad flagstop that is now a parking space south of US 2. The Air Line Trail goes straight up prominent Durand Ridge.

Take US 2 west from Gorham's traffic lights. Drive 5.5 miles over Gorham Hill and across Moose River. You identify Appalachia on the left (south) by the row of hikers' cars even before you see the signs "Trails Parking."

Facing the mountains, take the path from the right hand corner of the parking area. Cross the Boston and Maine tracks. The path forks, Valley Way bearing left, Air Line right. Keep to the right under the powerline. At the edge of the woods is a sign for Air Line. You enter maple woods. Various trails, for which you have seen signs, begin to branch from both sides of Air Line. You pass the Link and Amphibrach. Next, you pass the crossing of Sylvan Way, then later, Beechwood Way. Then Short Line branches right, and you cross Randolph Path, all in the first mile. Keep on Air Line.

The trail goes up soon enough. Expect an abrupt rise beyond a spring on your left off the trail. The steep and uneven section of the trail takes you up Durand Ridge. You pass the junction of Scar Trail coming in on the left, then after ½ mile you pass Upper Bruin; both trails connect to Valley Way in the valley of Snyder Brook.

Durand Ridge, reaching above treeline, sharpens to the Knife Edge. You clamber past rocks that overlook the precipitous King Ravine on your right.

From the Ravine comes a trail, Chemin des Dames ("Ladies' Road"), which is the "easy" way up from that mysterious giant gorge named for its 1857 explorer, the Reverend Starr King. You look down upon rocks the size of houses. Hidden in caves under them, ice never melts. The Ravine, by legend, is the resting place for a starving band of Rogers Rangers retreating after their retaliatory attack on the St. Francis Indian village in Canada during the French and Indian War.

Air Line next takes you past a branch trail, left, to AMC's Madison Hut, which is

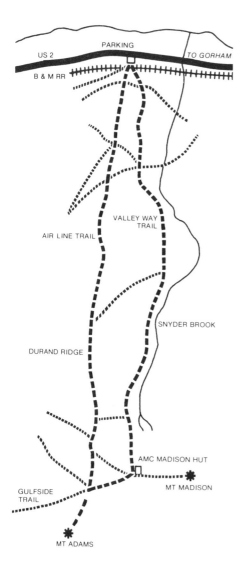

situated near the barren col between Mount Adams and Mount Madison. You keep on Air Line and climb steeply past the King Ravine Trail, right, at an entrance between ledges forming the Gateway into that glacial cirque.

Air Line joins the Gulfside Trail, coming in at the left, and they merge for a few yards. Mount Madison is in full view northeast.

(If you're caught by one of the notable Mount Adams thunderstorms, which feature virtuoso lightning bolts, and your hair seems inclined to stand on end, turn left onto Gulfside Trail for a descent to shelter at Madison Hut. Yellow-painted stones top Gulfside cairns.)

The Air Line Trail soon forks left off the Gulfside Trail. (Gulfside continues around Mount Adams toward Mount Jefferson and Mount Washington.) Air Line climbs past a minor summit, on the left, named John Quincy Adams for the sixth president, and takes you up among rock slabs to the main peak of Mount Adams.

The summit spreads out before you a tremendous view into the Great Gulf. You feel as though you were leaning over the abyss, not because of sheer cliffs but because of the vastness. Mount Washington's superior height and size dominate the south outlook; the summit buildings are three and one-half miles away. Across the Gulf on a winding ribbon up the slopes, small bugs, which are cars, creep along the auto road. At the horizon to your right, Mount Jefferson stands jagged against the sky; to your left, Mount Madison. Turning around northward, you see below you a lesser crest, named for the revolutionary of the Adams family—Sam Adams—and rising beyond is Thunderstorm Junction, where Gulfside Trail meets other trails at a huge cairn. In this north view on a clear day, you see the two bare Percy Peaks in the distance and the ridges near the Canadian border. More to the east, Umbagog

Mt. Adams, from Mt. Jefferson

Lake sparkles in the forest at the end of Maine's Rangeley Lakes chain.

For your descent, retrace your steps down Air Line as far as Gulfside Trail. Keep past the place where Air Line forks left and stay on Gulfside for the steep drop into evergreen scrub near Madison Hut. The Gulfside Trail ends at the hut.

Take Valley Way Trail for your return to Appalachia. Valley Way descends rapidly into the Snyder Brook valley and offers protection from storms after you enter the woods. Follow it past and across several trails, until it joins Air Line as you complete the loop and approach Appalachia.

Mount Madison

Distance (round trip): 10½ miles
Walking time: 8 hours
Vertical rise: 3,800 feet
Maps: USGS 7½' Carter Dome;
  USGS 15' Mt. Washington

This rock pyramid completes the Presidential Range's northern peaks. Tourists and hikers alike see its bare crags towering above the northern approach to Pinkham Notch. Of its 5,363 feet, 4,500 rise directly from the Androscoggin River valley. It juts above treeline into the alpine-arctic environment of fragmented rock slabs, cold fogs, wind and scanty vegetation. The peak is particularly impressive from NH 16 near the entrance to the Mount Washington Auto Road, where the Osgood Trail formerly began. Hikers for a hundred years enjoyed this scenic trail to Mount Madison's summit. They continue to do so, but from a new, 1985, parking area and an approach via the Great Gulf Trail.

Fine views on Osgood Ridge from treeline upward extend south and west into the Great Gulf, across to Mount Washington, and along the range that sweeps over Mount Jefferson and Mount Adams to Madison. The route of this hike includes not only Osgood Ridge and Mount Madison's summit, but also AMC's Madison Hut and a return loop through Madison Gulf. The climb should be saved for a shining clear day.

Drive 1.6 miles north of the entrance to the Auto Road. At a large sign for the

Great Gulf Wilderness turn west off NH 16. The parking area along the bank of the Peabody River was once the route of NH 16. With your pack equipped for a climb into the alpine-arctic zone, walk across the footbridge spanning the river.

The trail beyond the bridge leads up a slight grade among hemlocks to the Great Gulf Trail from Dolly Copp Campground two miles north of your car via NH 16. Turn left onto the Great Gulf Trail. Soon you will be walking above the rushing torrents and pools of the Peabody River's West Branch. At times the Great Gulf Trail coincides with sections of the Hayes Copp Ski Touring Trail from the campground.

The ski trail is blazed with small squares of blue plastic, not to be confused with blue paint blazes of the Great Gulf Trail. Three bridges and skier logo signs accommodate your brook crossings and direct you. Stay on the Great Gulf Trail.

After a mile of this pleasant woods walk your path bears away from the stream. You come to a junction of the ski trail branching north. In fifteen minutes more you arrive at the Osgood Trail on your right, also northward. This trail will be your route to Mount Madison. (The

Great Gulf Trail continues straight ahead.)

Turn right onto the Osgood Trail. You walk up an easy slope among beech and yellow birch, spruce and balsam. If you listen you can hear, down in the valley, the West Branch pouring over boulders and into pools.

Before the Osgood Trail takes you to serious climbing, it crosses a small brook and then brings you to an important junction. On your left the Osgood Cutoff enters. Take notice because you'll return here as you complete your loop from the Madison Gulf Trail via this Osgood Cutoff. (On your right, almost under a big boulder, a spur trail passes a spring, the last water, and ends at tent platforms.)

Continue ahead on the Osgood Trail. You can start climbing in earnest. This steep section must be dealt with by the patience formula; one boot in front of the other. You climb through fine spruce woods. You're on a section of the Appalachian Trail, and are also following the boundary of the White Mountain National Forest's 5,552-acre Great Gulf Wilderness.

The spruces diminish in size; they become sparse and scattered. You look up from your climbing and find yourself in the wind and skies among rocks that rise ahead crest after crest.

Pause here and try to predict the weather. Fierce gales blast Osgood Ridge, and storms come up rapidly. It's a long, rugged, unsheltered mile over a series of high rock piles. You can easily turn back here.

Fair skies and breezes are the signal to continue to climb up the craggy peaks. Follow the cairns among the rock slabs and over the ledges. You are on the

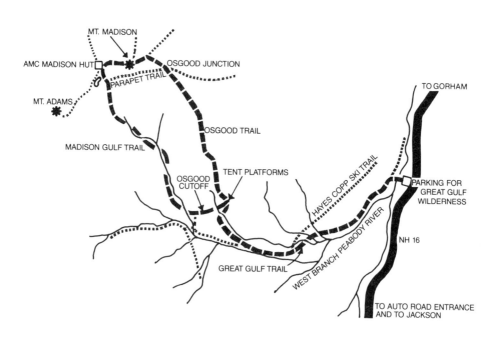

Moonrise over Mt. Madison

crest of Osgood Ridge, which curves left as well as up. You climb down a few yards over massive rocks to a narrow east-west flat. Trail signs mark this as Osgood Junction. The Daniel Webster Trail comes in on the right from Dolly Copp Campground. On the left, the Parapet Trail offers a one-mile circuit below Madison's summit to Madison Hut. (Very acceptable in a sudden rainstorm.)

The Osgood Trail goes up steeply again over the rocks along the ridge to Madison's northeast shoulder. It swings left down into a brief level section before the climb up the final pinnacle. On rising rocks again, you pass the Howker Ridge Trail, right. The Osgood Trail winds up westward among broken ledges.

At the summit, you stand on the big rocks that mark the end of the Presidential Range. The mountainside plunges northward into the valley. In that direction, the Watson Path drops off the summit. To the southeast you look down at the Auto Road entrance. Clouds may come pouring out of the northwest before you have studied Mount Washington and the cars rounding the auto road's corner called the Horn, which you see across the Great Gulf. Mount Adams on the west often catches cloud wisps or disappears entirely.

The return route begins on the summit as part of a loop into Madison Gulf. Keep west on the Osgood Trail along the jagged ridge beyond Madison's summit. The trail, marked by cairns, bears left off the ridge and descends the shoulder to Madison Hut below the looming crags of Mount Adams. The stone hut, where AMC hutmen provide meals and lodging for fifty hikers, serves also as a terminus for the Osgood Trail and various trails north and west.

Your route leaves the hut, south, by the Parapet Trail. Climb up the slope and keep left at the branch trail to tiny Star Lake. Across the col, Parapet Trail makes a sharp left turn as you approach the lookoff ledges. Then, it descends into a gully and the Madison Gulf Trail begins, right. (Parapet Trail keeps on toward Osgood Junction.) Turn right onto the Madison Gulf Trail. Climb down carefully over the steep, slippery rocks among scrub spruces.

The trail descends the Gulf by abrupt pitches between more gradual traverses, with many crossings of Parapet Brook. About 1½ hours from treeline, you make the last crossing over the brook's smooth rocks, to the east bank, and climb to a trail junction. Your route, the Osgood Cutoff, leads ahead toward the Osgood Trail. (The Madison Gulf Trail bears right down to the Great Gulf Trail.)

The Osgood Cutoff stays on a slabbing curve along the 2,500-foot contour through open woods. In about fifteen minutes you'll see the sign for the Osgood Trail junction. Turn right down the now familiar route to the Great Gulf Trail, where you turn left and continue to retrace the morning's path. Avoid the ski touring trail sections. Watch for the branch trail to the right leading to the suspension bridge. (The Great Gulf Trail keeps on to Dolly Copp Campground.)

Soon you can again admire the engineering of the bridge. Beyond it you'll welcome your car and its four wheels to carry you.

Mount Kearsarge North

Distance (round trip): 6 miles
Walking time: 5 hours
Vertical rise: 2,600 feet
Map: USGS 15' North Conway

If you start climbing Mount Kearsarge North at dawn and if the day stays clear, you'll see the shining wet rocks of Tuckerman Ravine's headwall sixteen miles north on Mount Washington; to the right, Lion Head's cliff glows, and Huntington Ravine's rock facade catches sunlight in a bright chasm.

Maps show the mountain as Kearsarge North, which distinguishes it from the Kearsarge near Warner. The former name, Mount Pequawket, is all but forgotten. The Pequawket Indians hunted and raised corn in the Conway-Fryeburg forests and meadows along the Saco River.

Mount Kearsarge North became a popular summit for white men after 1845, when three enterprising men cut a bridle path to the 3,268-foot top and built a two-story wooden inn. The structure survived many years until an autumn gale blew it loose from its iron mooring rods and chains. Rebuilt, it stood for twenty-five more years before the winds blew it apart. A 1951-vintage fire tower now occupies the summit ledge, but, like others in the mountains, it is no longer manned by a lone watcher; air patrols have taken over.

If you climb Mount Kearsarge North in the fall after snow has dusted the Presidentials, you'll understand the note on an eighteenth-century map issued during the French and Indian War, when this land was known only to hunters, trappers, and Indians. The note read "These WHITE HILLS appear many Leagues off at Sea like great bright Clouds above the Horizon, & are a noted Land Mark to Seamen."

Drive about 2 miles north from North Conway on NH 16. Pass the scenic outlook to Mount Washington. Cross the railroad tracks and turn right onto the Hurricane Mountain Road. Drive through Kearsarge Village. Less than .5 mile beyond, the Mount Kearsarge North Trail starts on the left at a trail sign and small parking area.

The trail enters the woods and traverses tree-grown fields of the former Eastman farm; once a shady lane led to the house and barn. Steven Eastman built this lower trail through his pasture about 1872 as a link to the bridle path at Prospect Ledge. Now the farm has returned to forest.

The true ascent begins after the first ½ mile. Steadily upward the trail progresses through hardwoods of maple, beech, and birch to open rocks sparsely grown to

View toward Mt. Kearsarge North

MT. KEARSARGE NORTH

MT BARTLETT

MT. KEARSARGE NORTH TRAIL

KEARSARGE BROOK

TO RTE 113

TO N.CONWAY AND NH 16

PARKING HURRICANE MT RD

KEARSARGE VILLAGE

sumacs and evergreens. You follow cairns and paint marks over slanting Prospect Ledge. There are wide views to the Saco valley south and west.

In the woods again and ½ mile farther, a good midway resting point, you come to a spring, down the bank to the right. (The summit is dry.) Climb on for another ½ hour along an ascending forest trail to more open ledges and scattered trees.

Gradually you pass the minor wooded summit, Mount Bartlett, on your left and swing north and east around ledges again. Turning south for the final climb, you follow cairns and worn paths up the last rocks among spruces to the summit ledge and tower. You first look straight ahead to Maine and its lakes. Then you turn left, and the Presidential Range takes all your attention.

Tom-Field-Avalon Loop

Distance (round trip): 8 miles
Walking time: 6 hours
Vertical rise: 2,800 feet
Map: USGS 15' Crawford Notch

Trails south from Crawford Notch link Mount Tom, Mount Field, and Mount Avalon for a loop hike. Spruces cloak Mount Field and Mount Tom, but both summits reach above 4,000 feet: Mount Tom, 4,047 feet, and Mount Field, 4,326 feet. Mount Avalon, a bare rock escarpment at 3,432 feet, overlooks Crawford Notch toward Webster Cliff and Mount Washington.

Drive to the site of the Crawford House on US 302 at the northern end of the Notch. East of this, and south of Saco Lake's west end, the old railroad depot is an information center maintained by the AMC, which acquired the land and remaining buildings around the Crawford House after it was dismantled and burned in 1977. Park near the depot. The Avalon Trail, your first section of the loop, begins across the Maine Central Railroad tracks south of the depot. Step over the tracks and cross a narrow, neglected field to the entrance into the woods.

Your loop hike will take you up the Avalon Trail to the A–Z Trail and Mount Tom Spur, then the Willey Range Trail to Mount Field, back down the Avalon Trail to Mount Avalon, and the return to your car at Crawford Depot.

A wide path through the woods, the Avalon Trail soon leads you past the trail on the left to Mount Willard, which offers less-ambitious members of a party a spectacular view for 1½ miles of upgrade. Shortly you come to the valley's brook and cross. Up the west bank you begin the real climb. You pass on your left the lower and upper junctions of a bypass trail for viewing cascades. A ledge farther on, and left, gives a breathing place above The Pool.

About half an hour from your car, the trail leads to the right, west of the old path higher on the bank, and takes you to the second crossing of the brook. You are climbing toward the steep end of the valley, which is essentially a glacial cirque with a wooded headwall. Many water bars and steps have been built into the trail. Watch for the A–Z Trail. It forks right on an ascent where the upper rim of the cirque appears in that direction. Take the A–Z Trail. (You will return to this junction as you near the end of your hike.)

The A–Z Trail drops into and climbs out of a rough gully, then angles up for ½ mile to the last trickling brook. You begin the steep, rough ½-mile climb that takes you up to the height-of-land be-

Spruce grouse

tween Mount Tom and Mount Field.

A spur trail leads right for the ¾-mile climb to Mount Tom's summit. It winds through a tunnel in the evergreens into young leafy trees alternating with spruce and fir. Blown-down evergreens on the north shoulder are being superseded by birch and poplar. You swing south to the summit, where the trail ends, ¾ mile from the A–Z Trail. A quiet lunch among Mount Tom's spruces and firs may reveal dark spruce grouse feeding toward you among the ferns and wood sorrel or pecking at the evergreen needles. The male sports a red eyebrow. In sunlight and shade his black and gray feathers hide him until he moves. This denizen of remote conifer forests is protected by New Hampshire law. His deliberate actions and lack of fear caused early hunters to think of domestic fowl and name him and his mate "fool hens."

After lunch, retrace your steps to the A–Z Trail and turn right. Follow it a short distance to the Willey Range Trail, which branches left toward Mount Field. (The A–Z Trail continues into the valley to join the Zealand Trail; thus its significance: Avalon to Zealand. For a description of the Zealand Trail see Hike 31.)

Through close growths of fir, spruce, and birch, you begin the 1 mile to Mt.

Field's summit. You emerge into more open woods and taller evergreens. Look behind you in the gaps between trees for views of Mount Tom. Keep on up the final pitch, passing the junction where the Avalon Trail descends, left. You reach the summit in another 100 yards. A small opening between dead or fallen spruce and fir affords a view south to Mount Carrigain and Carrigain Notch, also to Mount Hancock, North and South Twin, and more distant peaks, as well as the nearer Zealand Valley, westward.

To the north you walk across the trail and look over young evergreens toward the panorama of the summits south of Mount Washington—Eisenhower, Jackson, Webster, and Crawford Notch. Beyond Washington and its barren slopes below the buildings and towers, Mount Jefferson looks more remote and unspoiled.

Return to the Avalon Trail for the descent. It drops sharply down the side of Mount Field through low spruces. Care

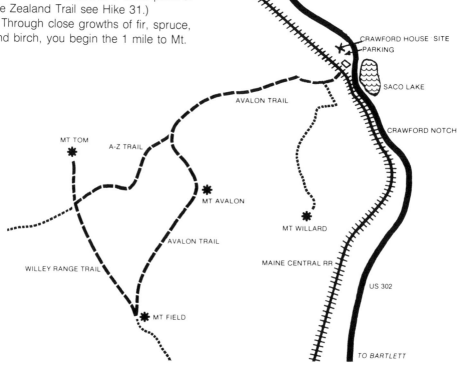

should be taken here: the footing on broken stones, wet turf, and occasional mud is often treacherous despite the stone and log steps. The flat shoulder leading toward Mount Avalon's rocks provides openings in the scrub for views north and east. Behind you Mount Field rises so abruptly you'll understand why you descended so quickly.

The main trail bypasses the crest of Mount Avalon, but a side trail leads to the right a few yards up the rocks for a bird's-eye view of Crawford Notch and the hotel site 1,500 feet below. Don't miss this lookoff because you are a bit weary. You'll see the highway parallel to the railroad winding through the Notch, one of the great passes of the Northeast. Webster Cliff is a stark mass of sheer rock buttressing the mountain northward. In the distance you gaze at the long Presidential Range centered on Washington's barren cone, which you identify by the buildings and broadcasting towers.

Below Mount Avalon, the trail continues to drop rapidly down through the spruces to the junction with the A–Z Trail, and the return to Crawford Depot and your car.

Mount Starr King/Mount Waumbek

Distance (round trip): 7½ miles
Walking time: 6 hours
Vertical rise: 2,600 feet
Map: USGS 15' Mt. Washington

A hiker in the White Mountains should see the Presidential Range from Mount Starr King. Thirteen miles northwest of Mount Washington across the upper valley of the Israel River, Starr King gives you a look at the complete panorama of the five rocky crests serrating the horizon eastward above the massed green slopes. From Mount Washington your eyes follow the skyline over Clay, Jefferson, Adams, and Madison.

In his 1859 book, the Reverend Thomas Starr King described the then-neglected views of the Presidentials from the north and northwest. He extolls Jefferson "Hill," which he says, "may without exaggeration be called the *ultima thule* of grandeur in the artist's pilgrimage among the New Hampshire mountains, for at no other point can he see the White Hills themselves in such array and force." The Reverend King gives no account of climbing summits north of present US 2, but his name is fittingly given to the mountain that is the great lookoff for studying and enjoying the northern slopes of the Presidentials.

On US 2 in Jefferson, drive .7 mile east from NH 116 junction to the site of the former Waumbek Inn. Turn north off the highway and follow a driveway leading uphill. Go left at a fork, then the next left. Drive carefully over water bars and past a concrete-walled sugar house. Bear right to park at the beginning of a bulldozed road, or on the left near a little reservoir and concrete dam.

The trail ascends straight up along an old logging road. You climb steadily through small hardwoods. Parallel on the left is the brook. You pass an old spring house on the right and then a pipe from a big spring up on the bank. Keep to the right at the fork not far above the pipe. In less than ½ mile, the trail turns right off the logging road and takes you up the mountain at an equable grade for ¾ mile. Then it jogs right and left again at a boundary stake. As you climb into the zone of spruce and fir toward 3,000 feet, you pass two springs on the trail's left slope. One fulfills all the requirements for an ideal cold spring; it trickles from under a ledge into a shallow pool. The trail swings around to the north as it continues up and up. It approaches the summit from that direction.

Spruces screen partial views from the ledges near the big cairn there. Proceed along the trail about 200 feet through the trees. You abruptly emerge into the clearing, and there before you, peak after

On Mt. Starr King

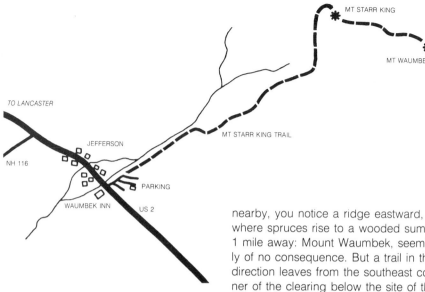

peak – the Presidentials!

Sunlight alternates with cloud shadows over the mountains. Often, mists gather around the rugged peaks of Mounts Adams and Washington. Binoculars bring out the Madison Hut at the col between Madison and Adams. You look into the depths of King Ravine on Adams. Watch for the train on the cog railway climbing Washington. Below your vantage point is the green valley of Israel River and Jefferson Meadows, and farther away you see wooded Cherry Mountain. The Franconia Range seems far away beyond numberless smaller mountains and ridges, but Lafayette's blue-green silhouette assures you that you're looking at Franconia Notch's giant. Your gaze inevitably returns to the main attraction, the Presidential Range.

When you finally look more to your left nearby, you notice a ridge eastward, where spruces rise to a wooded summit 1 mile away: Mount Waumbek, seemingly of no consequence. But a trail in that direction leaves from the southeast corner of the clearing below the site of the dismantled log shelter. It winds through the evergreens below the ridge, then ascends. Although roughly laid out among stumps and tree trunks, it is well worn by hikers adding another 4,000-foot mountain for their records. Mount Waumbek is higher than Starr King – 4,020 feet against 3,913.

Waumbek offers glimpses of the Presidentials through spruces at the end of a short trail past the summit sign on a tree. Clouds whirl turbulently overhead and gather around Mounts Adams and Madison. The appeal of Waumbek is primitive, a north-country wildness occasionally animated by small birds in the spruces – boreal chickadees and golden-crowned kinglets.

Return to the clearing on Starr King for a final scanning of the panorama before you, then descend through woods brightened by the lowering sun along the trail you climbed when the day was new.

Mount Eisenhower

Distance (round trip): 6½ miles
Walking time: 5 hours
Vertical rise: 2,725 feet
Maps: USGS 15′ Mt. Washington; USGS
  15′ Crawford Notch

Southwest from Mount Washington, rocky peaks extend toward Crawford Notch. One of these, Mount Eisenhower (former- ly Mount Pleasant), commands a spec- tacular view to all points of the compass.

This broad dome overlooks sections of the famous 8-mile Crawford Path from Crawford Notch. Three beeline miles to the north, past Mount Franklin's long hump and Mount Monroe's two crests, Washington pursues its role as the highest point in the Northeast: it hosts tourists carried to the top by cog railway and automobile; it supports the summit buildings, towers, and observatory; it tolerates—with occasional good weather—the many hikers on its exposed slopes.

Into the arctic-alpine world of Mount Eisenhower, the Edmands Path climbs up a west ridge and around the north base of the dome to the Crawford Path. There, near this junction, a side trail leads up the crags and over the rounded 4,761-foot summit. On a clear day, from that vantage point high above the forests, the sky and rocks are elemental and clean.

To reach the Edmands Path, turn off US 302 at Fabyan onto the Base Road leading to the cog railway's Base Station.

Soon Mount Eisenhower comes into sight as a hemispherical outline contrasting with its more jagged neighbors and topped by a tiny spike pricking the sky- line—actually a great cairn on the sum- mit. Drive on the Base Road about 5 miles to an intersection. Turn right. You are now on the Mount Clinton Road. Drive 1.5 miles from the four corners. And drive carefully; there's a startling 90-degree curve about .5 mile from the trail.

The Edmands Path enters the woods on the left, east, just north of the culvert over Assaguam Brook. The great trail builder, J. Rayner Edmands, relocated and graded the path in 1909. It bears left among beech and yellow birch. It crosses a footbridge over Abenaki Brook. Keep to the right up an old logging road beside the brook. You begin to climb somewhat here. Then the trail swings left up the ridge that will take you to treeline. The grade steepens but is nowhere ex- cessive. You enter spruce/fir woods, the habitat of the blackpoll warbler and Bicknells's thrush.

You climb up sections of graded fill held on the slope by rockwork. You notice rocks drilled and split with hand tools to clear and ease the way. In the

Mt. Eisenhower from Crawford Path

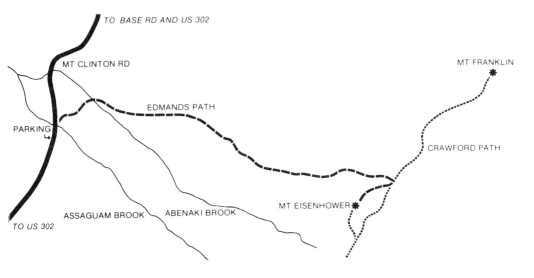

upper spruce/fir woods the trail crosses three seasonal source-streams of Mount Pleasant Brook; don't count on them for water. Approaching treeline among small birches and spruces, you find the trail paved with flat stones. These are almost unbelievable monuments to Edmands's meticulous trail construction.

If a cloud thick as sea fog masks the rocks, or if a storm threatens, heed the Forest Service warning sign in the last trees, and turn back.

Once above treeline, you will see that the Edmands Path splits into three gravel trails between ledges and across the alpine sward. Keep straight ahead up to the junction with the Crawford Path. Then turn right, south. After a few yards bear right again. This is the side trail over Mount Eisenhower whose rough dome rises ahead. (The Crawford Path bears left around the base.) You descend slightly and pass a little pool, Red Pond, on your left. Up the ragged ledges the trail zigzags, then takes you in a more gradual swing to the wide summit and

the great cairn. The green cushions all across the summit are the alpine plant, diapensia. If you climb in mid-June, you'll see the array of white blossoms.

Walk around for the views. To the north, up Mount Franklin curves the old and honored Crawford Path, in use for 160 years. Dropping away east of Mount Franklin, the ledges disappear into Oakes Gulf, where Dry River (Mount Washington River) begins its turbulent run to the Saco River. Beyond Mount Franklin, you see a small peak on the left and a higher crest right, which combine to form Mount Monroe. Then comes Washington, often crowned by a misty cloud.

Your return follows the same route to the Edmands Path junction with the Crawford Path. Turn left down to the graded way and into the trees. The construction so carefully carried out by J. Rayner Edmands makes the descent as nearly painless as your tired legs will experience anywhere. But this ease may trick you: it's likely to lull you so that the descent seems longer than the climb.

Mount Crawford

Distance (round trip): 5 miles
Walking time: 4½ hours
Vertical rise: 2,100 feet
Map: USGS 15' Crawford Notch

A rough oval of ledges around spruce scrub, Mount Crawford's 3,129-foot promontory extends into the broad delta of ridges and valleys that flow ten miles south from Mount Washington. Two great cliffs, one and one-half miles northeast, the Giant Stairs, identify Stairs Mountain and the long, forested Montalban Ridge. The Presidential Range's southern peaks appear at the far north end of the Dry River valley. To the northwest, Mount Willey looms over Crawford Notch.

A former bridle path, cut fifteen years before the Civil War, passes east of Mount Crawford to Mount Washington. (A spur path rises to Mount Crawford's summit.) This route, called the Davis Path, was constructed by Nathaniel Davis, proprietor of the Mount Crawford House, and brother-in-law of the famous Ethan Allen Crawford. Nathaniel Davis sold his horses about the time adventurous sightseers began riding up the Carriage Road being built from the Glen House in Pinkham Notch. After 1855 the bridle path fell into disuse and grew back to woods. In 1910, the AMC and volunteers reopened it, discovering, with the aid of a Maine woodsman, all the original path.

To make this historic and rewarding hike, drive about 6 miles west from Bartlett on US 302. Watch for a stone house known as "The Inn Unique" on the left above a railroad crossing for old US 302, now bypassed. You are at Notchland, which was once a station named Bemis, for the builder of the stone house. A short distance beyond this, turn right into a large parking area. The Davis Path begins at the northwest corner along a rough roadway leading to the suspension footbridge over the shallow Saco River.

Beyond the bridge you enter an open field. The trail keeps to the north edge adjacent to a wide lawn and house on your right. At an AMC sign follow a path into bushes and alders. It takes you to a pair of logs over a muddy brook channel. At the opposite bank, turn right at once. Disregard a path straight ahead up the bank. Your trail keeps along the brook to a former crossing now flooded by beavers. Keep straight on above the brook for about 100 yards. Then the trail jogs sharply left. You walk through open woods and across a dry brook bed with smooth stones, which takes the spring overflow from the running brook you soon cross. This is the last water.

You begin the climb along the old bridle path. For a time the trail swings around to the left, avoiding an extensive

Near Mt. Crawford

area of windfalls, many of which have been chopped from the trail. The steady grade and occasional log steps return you to the bridle path. You climb more steeply on straight stretches dug from the slope and supported on your left by rock retaining walls which Nathaniel Davis built for permanence. You wonder at the strong backs and patience of the men who worked with oxen, chains, and crowbars. The graded trail reminds you of the untold miles of New England's stone walls.

You follow winding turns as you approach the top of the ridge. You emerge from spruces on open ledges, where you look northwest to Crawford Notch and Mount Willey. Keep right, over two wave-like swells and across an arm of spruce woods to rock again. Watch for cairns ahead and white paint marks on the ledges among scattered spruces.

You come to a long slanting rock face. There is a white, T-shaped blaze on the base of the rock indicating the spur. A sign to your left and one to your right are for the Davis Path. Walk between their trees and up the rock face.

At the top, the path continues among ledges and spruces, marked by a few cairns. The paint blazes on the rocks have faded, but the trail stays on the ridge crest, and about ¼ mile from the Davis Path you step out on the cliff that looks off to the Giant Stairs and the

gravel slides of Montalban Ridge. Ledges continue around a small growth of spruces, with views up Dry River — misnamed because it can be a turbulent, dangerous stream — to Mount Eisenhower, Mount Franklin, Mount Monroe, and Mount Washington. Walk around and look southwest to Mount Carrigain and its tower. To your left, down in the valley, you see the stone house and the highway. Mount Crawford gives you a complete 360-degree panorama for your 2½-mile climb.

Giddy from mountain vistas, you may for a change turn to the tiny cranberry vines clinging to rock crevices along with alpine crowberry. Labrador tea and blueberries grow in the shelter of the five-foot spruces. White-throated sparrows flit nearby. Cedar waxwings perch on dead twigs and survey the scene in their alert way. This is a place to linger, to look about again, and to eat a hearty lunch.

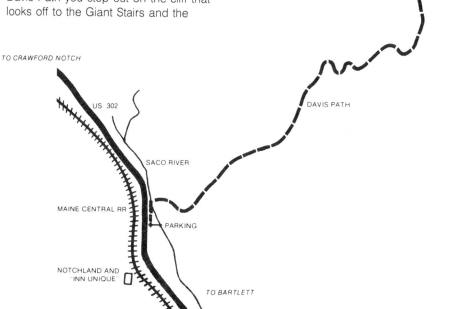

MT CRAWFORD

TO CRAWFORD NOTCH

US 302

DAVIS PATH

SACO RIVER

MAINE CENTRAL RR

PARKING

NOTCHLAND AND "INN UNIQUE"

TO BARTLETT

Backpacking
Hikes

Mount Hancock

Time allowed: 2 days, 1 night
Distance (round trip): 9½ miles
Walking time (with pack for 5½ miles): 7½ hours
Vertical rise (including both peaks): 2,400 feet
Maps: USGS 7½′ Mt. Osceola; USGS 15′ Crawford Notch

Your first overnight hike should test, but *gently*. It should give you the chance to try out new boots, pack, tent, cooking kit, and food—and, most important, your own capacity. But it should not include too many miles. The trip to Mount Hancock meets these specifications.

The Hancock Notch Trail goes north from the Kancamagus Highway at the hairpin turn about 10.5 miles east of Lincoln. Off the upper half of the hairpin is a parking area.

The trail follows a logging railroad grade through young hardwoods merging with spruce and fir as you swing east above Hancock Branch's North Fork. The grade curves around the west shoulder of Mount Huntington at about the 2,300-foot contour. In places, swampy ground nurtures lush sphagnum moss at either side of the packed fill. The rails have been gone since before World War I. Rows of blasted rocks still hold the fill in place. Cuts through ledge and banks are ten and twelve feet deep. The fast, easy walking is interrupted at gullies and brooks once spanned by log bridges.

Hardly fifteen minutes from the Kancamagus Highway a sign on a tree notifies you that you are entering a Restricted Use Area. No camping, no wood or charcoal fires within ¼ mile of the stream or trail. As you walk by various tent sites with stone rings for campfires, often abandoned with unburned trash and tin cans left behind, surrounded by packed soil and hacked stumps, you'll understand the reason for the RUA. Camping repeatedly in places destroys vegetation and landscape.

You walk in this RUA for thirty to forty minutes. It ends at the Cedar Brook Trail branching left, northward, in spruce and balsam woods. You are 1¾ miles from the highway. (The Hancock Notch Trail continues east to the height-of-land and down to Sawyer River, which drains into the Saco River south of Crawford Notch.)

Camping beyond the RUA, however, should be at least 200 feet from the trail or brook. Don't pitch your tent on a site that's been used. Find your own. More about this when you are nearer the mountain.

Turn to the left across a little brook and begin the climb up Cedar Brook Trail. The name derives from the brook on the far side of Mount Hitchcock, which is ahead and to your left, west of north. Mount Hancock is ahead and to the right, hidden like Hitchcock by trees. You are still following Hancock Branch's North

Fork. You cross it five times in the next ¾ mile.

The brook takes on a rusty color. An old beaver pond, peat bogs, spruces, and tamaracks give the tan shade to the water. You follow the trail through a mossy bog where pitcher plants—those strange insect-eaters—grow near heavy turf interlaced with rootlets. The old logging road is wide, and the bog beyond the last crossing is churned by hiker's boots.

Watch on the right for the Hancock Loop Trail. It cuts into thicker woods as a wide aisle from the open, wet area, and soon takes you across the brook to an overused campsite of bare earth, stone campfire circles—and, after rain, mud. Don't bother to look for a place to pitch your tent. There, too, hikers have camped repeatedly. Seek your own site by continuing up the trail. It becomes a minor brook (sometimes dry) through jumbled rocks for a few yards. Next comes a boggy section partially spanned by stepping stones and log walkways. After ten minutes from the overused campsite begin looking for your own private place.

I suggest as a landmark in a likely area the group of three big boulders to your left across the brook. You'll want to avoid two sites close to the water and already showing the wear and tear of thoughtless campers. Scout around above the big rocks or on the south side of the trail. You need only an opening large enough for your tent. Alternatively, you may climb farther up the trail as it rises above the brook and from there descend to level camping areas in the valley.

Along here you have carried your pack about 3 miles—far enough to have learned some packing tricks and trials, far enough to have felt, at least briefly, the exhilaration of carrying your home with you, the freedom of the backpacker.

The light nylon tent goes up quickly.

Or it does if you've practiced in your back yard or even in your living room. Fluff out the down-filled sleeping bag. The traditional campfire may wait until you have cooked your freeze-dried meal on a backpacker's gasoline stove. Then a very small fire on bare ground (as your fire permit requires) warms and cheers as darkness approaches. It may also attract white-footed mice hopping delicately near. Later, when you're dropping off to sleep, they will rustle in the pack's food bags if you left them on the ground, and you will have to wriggle out of your bag to hang the pack in a tree by flashlight, bare feet cold in the dew.

Next morning prepare for a day hike. Beyond your camp, Hancock Loop Trail is still on the old logging road that parallels the valley on your left. The steady climb in young hardwoods and evergreens lifts you up to glimpses of the slide identifying Mount Hancock's south slope. It's a slippery-looking face of bedrock granite, at a distance smooth as gray glass above a jumble of rocks and gravel. Early ascents were made up the slide, a dangerous route now replaced by the wooded trail. You are now far above the brook. You come to the junction for the loop over Mount Hancock's two summits. To your left the valley drops away to a gully and source of the brook—usually dry in summer—and to the base of the slide.

Both summits are more than 4,000 feet high, yet wooded. To climb the 4,403-foot north peak first—although the order chosen matters little—turn left down into the dry brook gully. The trail bears right, away from the slide's base, and enters the spruces. You climb up very steeply, but avoid the slide as the trail is cut up through the woods. Despite the angle, much larger spruces once grew here. You rest at monster stubs and fallen trunks, some charred from forest fire. One stub, three feet through at the

Backpacking near Mt. Hancock

butt, towers above the new growth.

From the north peak, which you reach at an opening in the spruces near the summit sign, you may turn left to the head of the slide for a view toward the mountains around Waterville Valley, Mount Osceola and some of the Sandwich Range. Return to the summit and walk along the loop trail less than a hundred yards. A spur trail on your right leads to "Plymouth Rock." It resembles the original. Spruces have grown up around it and cut off striking views of

Mount Washington and Mount Carrigain.

Leaving the north peak summit, the trail descends along the crest of the ridge and turns southeast on a narrow

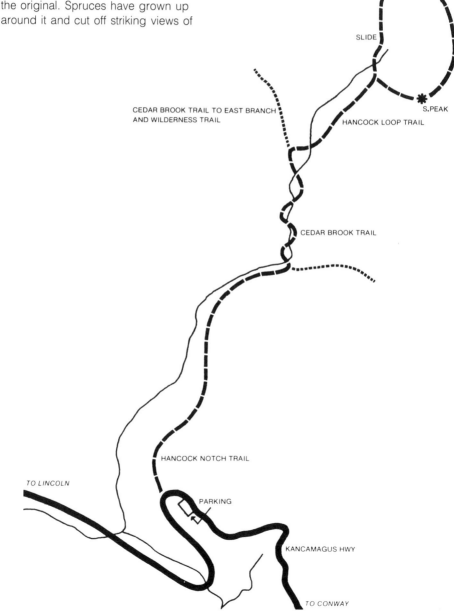

winding traverse up and down, around blowdowns, and across surprising wet spots. The trail gradually ascends the south peak to 4,274 elevation. An opening a few yards east gives you an outlook over the Sawyer River valley.

Beyond the south peak, the trail turns right, west, and drops sharply away down through spruce/fir woods to the end of the logging road that returns you to the junction where you began the loop. Of the total distance around the loop, 2¼ miles, all but the ridge mile has been up or down as steeply as almost any trail in the mountains, which explains the three hours it requires.

Retracing your earlier steps to camp, you have time for another meal before folding up the tent and packing for the hike out. Douse your fire twice and stir the ashes—if you bothered with a fire. A backpacker's stove is faster and safer than cooking on a wood fire. Restore the site to its natural wildness, even to brushing up the duff flattened under your tent and sleeping mat; use a dead branch. And of course carry out all your trash.

For the return trip, one and one-half hours should be enough time—less, if you stride down the railroad grade like a veteran backpacker.

Sandwich Mountain

Time allowed: 2 days, 1 night
Distance: 13 miles
Walking time: 9½ hours
Vertical rise: 2,500 feet
Maps: USGS 15′ Plymouth; USGS 15′ Mt. Chocorua

Viewed from a distance, the heavy silhouette that terminates the Sandwich Range's western reach contrasts with the much-photographed eastern pinnacle, Mount Chocorua. Sandwich Mountain rises massively from a broad foundation buttressed by ridges extending from Waterville Valley south to Beebe River and east to Flat Mountain Ponds. On the west, it slopes to Black Mountain above Sandwich Notch. Spruce/fir woods grow to the 3,993-foot summit, but ledges offer partial outlooks. On this hike, the climb up Black Mountain from the west provides the spectacular views lacking on Sandwich Mountain.

First Day

Sandwich Notch Road to Sandwich Mountain to Black Mountain Pond Shelter

Distance: 7½ miles
Walking time: 6 hours

This big day of the trip includes all your climbing. From Campton, drive east on the Waterville Valley Road (NH 49) about 3.5 miles to a right turn, south, onto the Sandwich Notch Road. Follow this narrow, steep, dirt road 3.8 miles to the Algonquin Trail, which begins on the left

(northeast) side as a logging road. There is no designated parking here. Pull off the road and shoulder your pack.

The Algonquin Trail follows the logging road almost a mile, then branches left up toward the south face of Black Mountain. Climbing steadily among birches and beeches, it levels along the first bare rock and heath-like openings. Beyond a little seasonal brook you climb again abruptly to a col between a rocky knoll on your left and the main mountain ahead to the right. The next several pitches are difficult sections for the backpacker. In the evergreens you'll face one mass of creviced bedrock where you may decide to take off packs and pass them up.

The reward for this climb is a rocky lookoff into Sandwich Notch. The Sandwich Notch Road has been in use from the early days of settlement and once was bordered by farms and houses. From this viewpoint the trail turns back into thicker evergreens, then open rock with scrub growth here and there on the ridge leading to the summit.

The Algonquin Trail continues to a junction with the Black Mountain Pond Trail coming in from the right. The shelter on the pond is your destination for the night. Since you will return to this junction, you'll want to cache your pack here, taking along in one of those neat little nylon packs a canteen, lunch, and jacket. From this junction you have a 1¾-mile spur that will take you over Black Mountain and up Sandwich Mountain.

Continue east on the Algonquin Trail. It crosses a ledge from which you look down at Black Mountain Pond 1,000 feet below. Swinging somewhat left and entering spruces, you climb to Black Mountain's summit. Sometimes moose spend a winter on Black Mountain. Watching the trail, and startled by droppings apparently left by a pony herd, you may not at first realize you're walking through a moose "yard." So dense are the spruce

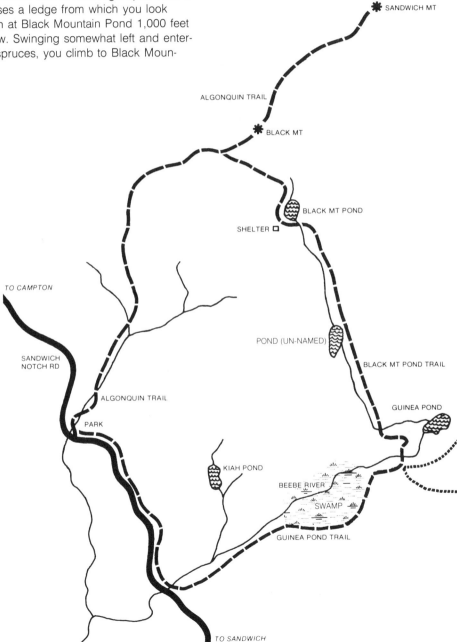

Lunch on Sandwich Mountain

and fir trees that moose find winter quarters under the protecting branches and food from the evergreen tips. Winter at 3,460 feet suits New Hampshire moose. Snow, crusting upper boughs, roofs a sheltered stable for the huge animals.

The Algonquin Trail now descends to the ridge that leads to Sandwich Mountain. You pass occasional ledges and outlooks north, but mostly you ascend through spruce/fir woods. The Algonquin Trail joins the Sandwich Mountain Trail for the last few yards to the summit. (The Sandwich Mountain Trail comes in, left, from the Waterville Valley Road.) The spruces hide much of the view, but from rocks near the large summit cairn you get a lookout over Waterville Valley to Mount Tecumseh's ski slopes and Mount Osceola's tower.

Retrace your route via the Algonquin Trail to the junction with the Black Mountain Pond Trail and your pack. Turn left (south) for the descent to the pond and shelter. The way is steep. Watch your footing and dig your heels in when gravity begins to get the best of you. The ledges and evergreens seem about to slide into the valley, yet they will probably stay in place. The tops of lower trees are on your eye level; you may have a close introduction to tiny golden-crowned kinglets. Approaching the base of this precipitous mountainside you descend through spruce woods that have never been cut. The trail levels out at beaver dams on the inlet to Black Mountain Pond. At the pond, the trail swings around the west shore, where you come to the open-front log shelter for eight hikers. The six-acre pond is thirty-two feet deep, clear, and the home of speckled trout.

Second Day

Black Mountain Pond Shelter to Sandwich Notch Road

Distance: 5½ miles
Walking time: 3½ hours

Easy walking this day leaves you free to swim and lie in the sun all morning. The pond is a gathering spot for birds and animals. Kingfishers, cedar waxwings, blackbirds, and ducks may be seen. In the spruces, white-throated sparrows flit about, and red squirrels scold.

From the shelter you look back up the steep slope you came down, and feel pleased that you don't have to climb it.

After lunch, pack shouldered once more, you leave the shelter and follow the Black Mountain Pond Trail above the south shore. The trail descends, crosses the outlet brook below rocks, turns right, and keeps to the east bank of the brook on a downhill slant along an old logging road. After about a half-hour the trail crosses some low, wet ground. You pass a small beaver pond on your right. The trail again descends gradually. The stream — still the outlet of Black Mountain Pond — flows into an extensive beaver pond of still water and dead trees. This has flooded the trail along the old logging road. An arrow on a tree and yellow blazes direct you around to the left, east. At the high and interesting dam on your right, keep below it to the outlet. There you step across and turn sharp left downstream to rejoin the logging road. Turn right and continue until another bypass, left, takes you around more boggy ground. This rough trail leads you to the crossing of Beebe River, here a brook. On the far side, after a short distance, the Black Mountain Pond Trail ends at the Guinea Pond Trail. Turn right on the Guinea Pond Trail for the Sandwich Notch Road. The Mead Trail, straight ahead at this junction, leads south up Mount Israel.

The Guinea Pond Trail follows the grade of a former logging railroad. This shaded avenue ends at open country, swamps, and a series of beaver dams backing up Beebe River. The flooded railroad grade ahead appears as a long pool through bushes and tall grass. To the right a more recent gravelly logging road will help identify this clearing. No sign. Turn left into the woods along a trail up to higher ground. It loops around the water and descends to the railroad grade. The swamp on your right is also a thicket of typical bushes, such as witherod and black alder. A locked swing-gate of heavy pipe bars vehicles. You enter woods as the grade becomes a wide jeep road. Level, it passes along a power line, left, then under it in the open as you descend to the Sandwich Notch Road. Turn right (north) over the bridge across Beebe River. Follow the dirt road north about 1½ miles to the beginning of the Algonquin Trail and your car.

East Branch Region/Mount Carrigain

Time allowed: 3 days, 2 nights
Distance (round trip): 28 miles
Walking time: 21 hours
Vertical rise: 3,300 feet
Maps: USGS 15′ Crawford Notch; USGS 7½′ South
    Twin Mtn.; USGS 7½′ Mt. Osceola

A three-day weekend is ideal for this hike. You exchange your daily routine in the modern world for life in the remote Pemigewasset "Wilderness" between Crawford Notch and the Franconia Range. The pleasures of distant woods and high mountains, as well as the satisfaction of backpacking and hiking nearly 30 miles in three days, may escape you unless you've walked enough to toughen your legs. On the morning after the first day's 7-mile hike through Carrigain Notch, you'll want to rise from your sleeping bag eager for 13 miles exploring the trails to Shoal Pond and Thoreau Falls. And you'll really enjoy the trip if your legs still have plenty of spring in them for the third day's climb up 4,680-foot Mount Carrigain.

For each of the three days, there are unique experiences to anticipate. First, Carrigain Notch, a true hikers' pass between mountain and cliff, opens to the headwaters of the Pemigewasset River's East Branch, where you camp at Desolation Shelter. Second, in those secluded valleys you find miles of first-class walking because old logging railroads provide easy grades beside clear streams. Third, Mount Carrigain's summit surprises you as a triangulation point for the great

ranges, and the splendid panorama draws all the mountains together into a coherent pattern.

Mount Carrigain's tower on the third day is the hike's culmination before you descend to your car and to civilization.

First Day

Carrigain Notch and Desolation Shelter

Distance: 7 miles
Walking Time: 6 hours

You start your trip with a backpack into the wilds through Carrigain Notch. Drive west about 4 miles from Bartlett on US 302. Cross the bridge over Sawyer River and turn left onto the Sawyer River Road. On the right, 2 miles in, a small parking place accommodates cars at the start of the Signal Ridge Trail, which serves as a way to the Carrigain Notch Trail.

Shouldering your pack, you climb up Signal Ridge Trail by a logging road across Whiteface Brook, which pours through its little valley on your right as you climb the first ridge. The trail swings west away from the stream, and you enter a logged area. Avoid the side roads. After one hour or so from the car, you approach Carrigain Brook. The Carrigain Notch Trail forks right. Signal Ridge Trail bears left. Turn right onto Carrigain Notch Trail. (On the third afternoon you'll descend Signal Ridge Trail from Mount Carrigain's summit to this junction.)

Now you head north along the Carrigain Notch Trail and soon cross Carrigain Brook. The trail leads toward Vose Spur, which is ahead and to your left but mostly out of sight above the hardwood forest. The trail's easy route stays a considerable distance west of the brook. Two bypasses on your right approach the brook to avoid two beaver ponds on tributaries. Under Vose Spur your boots will teeter over rounded cobblestones of several dry washes from the mountainside—incongruous under the big trees but indicative of spring freshets.

At the base of the Notch a clearing opened by a former beaver pond gives a view of the Notch's cliffs. Keep to the left along a bypass around the debris left by the beavers. It takes you to the steep climb among spruces and birches to the pass at an elevation of 2,639 feet.

Wild and unknown to many travelers, Carrigain Notch forms a gateway to the East Branch valley. On your left, a towering shoulder, Vose Spur, separates you from Mount Carrigain's main bulk. On the right, Mount Lowell rises above the cliffs that complete the gunsight formation of the Notch. The trail crosses beneath these heights among rocks and young spruces.

Dropping down over rocks and roots but more gradual than on the south slopes, the trail winds to an old logging road, which you can identify by rocks blasted into star shapes. The woods remain predominantly evergreens. You cross Notch Brook near its source and discover yet another bypass trail off to the left of the logging road's boggy sections. Your westerly direction is taking

you north of Mount Carrigain and south of Notch Brook, until you descend to a railroad embankment and a junction with the Nancy Pond Trail joining from the right. (The Nancy Pond Trail comes from Crawford Notch and US 302.)

Turn left for the continuation of the Carrigain Notch Trail along the railroad grade. For a mile you walk through evergreens, which open up at the site of vanished Camp 20 and a trail junction. The Carrigain Notch Trail turns abruptly right, downhill. Straight ahead and across a brook, the Desolation Trail begins. Its name refers to the devastation once caused by logging. (From this junction on the third day, you'll climb Desolation Trail to Mount Carrigain's summit.)

Your first day's hike is almost complete, and you may rest or explore here at old Camp 20. It's typical of many deserted East Branch logging sites that have returned to woods. Built by J. E. Henry and Sons Company of Lincoln, this Camp 20 remains only as rotted boards grown over by raspberry bushes. A dump hidden under forest duff contains rusty tin cans, old peavey ferrules, sled runners, and pieces of cast iron stoves. In 1912 the clearing was alive with hustling men and horses working in the woods from daylight until dark. Trains carried away the logs. Now, most hikers scarcely pause in walking by.

One hiker did. He tells of discovering evidence of toil and poverty. Near the dump he unearthed a rotted leather boot that had been resoled four times. Nails held leather to leather on this relic, and attested to a lumberjack's "making do" his only pair of boots. Yet the hiker recalled that many old lumberjacks look back upon their younger days in the camps and forests as the best years of their lives. (Rough on the forests, however.)

Turn right at Camp 20 as the Carrigain Notch Trail heads toward Desolation Shelter ¼ mile away, where you'll be spending the night. Situated among spruces, which provided its three log walls, the shelter opens toward a fireplace of rocks and a clearing above a boulder-strewn brook of transparent water—Carrigain Branch.

The water, however, may not be as pure as it looks because one of its sources is Carrigain Pond. You've heard about the unfortunate exchange between humans and beavers—*Giardia lamblia* (See Introduction.) For your drinking water at Desolation Shelter, walk back up the trail and watch for the tributary on the left, north, of its union with Carrigain Branch coming down from the south. This is the same brook you saw at Camp 20 and the beginning of the Desolation Trail.

The shelter sleeps eight hikers, and often attracts more than you'd guess from its remote location. When the shelter is occupied, a tent can be pitched nearby. (There may be a caretaker and a small fee.)

Second Day

Loop to Stillwater Junction, Shoal Pond, Thoreau Falls, East Branch, and back to Desolation Shelter

Distance: 13¾ miles
Walking time: 8½ hours

This walk along railroad grades and old haul roads benefits from an early start, which lengthens the day. Besides, as the sun begins to rise, you walk along the trail through cool woods; leaves and grass shine with dew, and the birds are singing.

For this loop you should leave your overnight equipment at the shelter or at your nearby tent site. Set aside lunch, water, rain gear, extra shirt—your usual necessities for a day hike—in a little pack or fanny pack. Place all remaining food in a strong bag and hang it out of reach

on a tree. Without your overnight equipment, of course, you also leave behind your backpacker's freedom. You might want to camp somewhere along the loop. If you decide to do this, evaluate the additional weight, and the mileage to complete the loop on the third day in distance and time, which I've not included. Mount Carrigain from the west is STEEP! You may want to stay another day if you treat the loop as a backpack, instead of as a day-hike.

From Desolation Shelter the Carrigain Notch Trail goes ½ mile down to its end at Stillwater Junction. Here you will find three trails joining. On your right, north, the Shoal Pond Trail leads at once across Anderson Brook. It will be your route for the morning. On your left, south, the Wilderness Trail begins as a curving bypass of the railroad grade, which lies straight ahead, thus avoiding two river crossings once spanned by trestles, but now difficult if not impossible. (The Wilderness Trail then parrallels the East Branch below Stillwater, on or above the south bank. It will be your afternoon's return route back to Stillwater Junction.)

Now from the spruces at Stillwater Junction you take the north route, Shoal Pond Trail, across the brook, aided by the concrete of a former dam. On the far side turn left on the railroad grade for a few yards, then follow the blue blazes to the grade that takes you straight for ½ mile through the new forest of poplar, wild cherry, white birch, yellow birch, and maple to the first crossing of Shoal Pond Brook. This is one of several bridgeless crossings in the 3½ miles to Shoal Pond.

During logging days before World War I, standard-gauge steam locomotives chugged along the steel rails and crossties, that were later taken up, rotted, or burned. The stocky, tough little locomotives towed flatcars from Lincoln with men and supplies for the camps, and, when necessary as the trees were cut back, moved the camps themselves. The trains also carried Sunday excursionists, for a fee, and trout fisherman. The work trains returned to Lincoln piled high with spruce logs from landings along East Branch and such tributaries as Shoal Pond Brook.

The Shoal Pond Trail takes advantage of one of these landings near the site of Camp 21. These platforms stored logs for the trains and were manned by a gang of men wielding peaveys.

The scene now at the site of Camp 21 is quiet and verdant. Only worn sled runners protruding from the leaves on the

ground, and cans from a dump, show that the camp ever existed. To the right in the brook a large, shallow pool collects water flowing over nearly-level ledge. Upstream the railroad grade ends, and you cross to the east bank. You follow old sled roads over log corduroy or often on modern trail walkways of split logs. The Shoal Pond Trail leads through part of the 18,560-acre Lincoln Woods Scenic Area set aside by the Forest Service in 1969 to remain safe from axe, saw, and bulldozer.

A young forest grows on the earth scorched by logging and fire. You walk in the shade of innumerable trees. Under National Forest protection since the early 1930s, this East Branch country has made a miraculous recovery. The wonder of returning forest speaks loud and clear for conservation, yet might suggest to the thoughtful hiker that earth and nature have given man more reprieves than he deserves.

Crossing to the west bank of the brook, you are approaching the pond through evergreens. The trail curves eastward again into more open country. Corduroy logs have been preserved by the cold and acid bog water. The land rises to dry ground. Midway on the east of the pond shore you can walk from the spruces to the water's edge, for a view of Mount Bond, west, and Whitewall Mountain, north.

A few hundred yards beyond the pond, the trail splits. Both forks lead to the Ethan Pond Trail. Take the left fork, which follows the old Zealand Notch railroad grade. This was another J. E. Henry enterprise that ended with fierce fires in 1886. Burned to bedrock, Whitewall Mountain north of you stands as testimony to the blazing inferno.

About ¾ mile from Shoal Pond, you reach the Ethan Pond Trail, where the Shoal Pond Trail ends. Keep left onto the Ethan Pond Trail.

For the purpose of this hike, the Ethan Pond Trail provides a ½-mile transfer to the Thoreau Falls Trail. (The Ethan Pond Trail comes from US 302 in Crawford Notch.) You follow the Ethan Pond Trail along the railroad grade to a footbridge over the East Branch's North Fork. Next, after about ¼ mile, you come to the Thoreau Falls Trail on your left. This is your 5-mile return route south along North Fork into the East Branch valley. (The Ethan Pond Trail goes north through Zealand Notch to the Zealand Trail near AMC's Zealand Falls Hut.)

Take the Thoreau Falls Trail, left. You are in a Restricted Use Area: no camping or fires. Soon you see the need— bare ground, scattered trees growing through compacted earth. But the spruce forest will in time recover from too many campers. Descending to the ledges and the brook, you find an ideal lunch spot. Thoreau Falls and noontime come together if the day's hike is proceeding on schedule. The North Fork cascades down the slanting rock into a deep ravine. Named, of course, for the author of *Walden*, the white water glints in the sun and is visible to hikers on the western ridge, where Mount Bond, the highest summit in the area at 4,174 feet, extends north to Mount Guyot, and Zealand Ridge curves along the northern horizon to Zeacliff.

After lunch you will have 7½ miles of afternoon walking back to Desolation Shelter. The Thoreau Falls Trail continues from the steep bank beyond the head of the cascade. Care and caution are required due to slippery rock. Sometimes the flow of water will force you to retreat upstream in search of a less dangerous crossing.

Once on the far side you climb the bank, then pick your way down a precipitous, muddy, rooty drop as the trail descends into the ravine. The trail remains rough along the east side of the

The East Branch of the Pemigewasset

valley until you come to the sled road used by J. E. Henry and Sons' loggers when they began cutting the first-growth spruce in 1916. The trail improves as the valley opens out, and notably so when it meets the end of the old railroad grade and follows it.

You come to a crossing of the North Fork. A bypass trail for use in time of highwater leads off to your left. Staying on the main trail, you descend to a beaver pool and cross on a log before you step out at the stream. Stones during low water levels provide a route across to the railroad grade and Jumping Brook, which pours in from the west. It, too, must be crossed on stones.

Below Jumping Brook, the grade passes the memorial plaque commemorating the deaths of Dr. Miller and Dr. Quinn of Hanover who died after a plane crash in February 1959. Farther downstream in about twenty minutes you come to the final crossing of North Fork. It will test your ability to leap from boulder to boulder. On the east bank at your left the highwater bypass rejoins the main trail.

Now you're all set for an hour's easy walking to the East Branch and a footbridge laid on sixty-foot logs. Look upstream for a good view of Mount Carrigain. Beyond the bridge you'll think the trail is leading you away from your correct eastern, upstream direction back to Desolation Shelter. It is. The trail follows the railroad grade for almost half a mile southwesterly to meet the Wilderness Trail at North Fork Junction.

Turn sharp left onto the Wilderness Trail. The gradual slope yet seems steep for an engine with cars behind it. After about fifteen minutes the trail leaves the grade to stay on the south bank instead of crossing as the railroad once did. This bypass winds along the bank and through Crystal Brook, then down to the grade, which has returned to the south

near the clearing at the site of Camp 18. Past the field of grass and fireweed some distance south of the East Branch, the trail stays on the grade until it meets the river again, and crosses. You need not. A more recent section of the Wilderness Trail takes you around two former difficult crossings. Stay on the grade to its end and step into the woods by this trail. It curves to the south of Stillwater, crosses Carrigain Branch, and returns you to Stillwater Junction for the completion of your day's loop. Turn to the right onto the Carrigain Notch Trail and retrace your morning walk to Desolation Shelter.

Third Day

Mount Carrigain via Desolation Trail and Signal Ridge Trail

Distance: 7¼ miles
Walking time: 6½ hours

If the weather is fair on this day of the climb up Mount Carrigain, you are in luck. If clouds and rain have descended, I suggest you go back to your car through Carrigain Notch and save the mountain for a clear day. You can see the summit from the brook bed above the shelter. Take a look and make your decision.

Shoulder your pack and walk up the Carrigain Notch Trail from the shelter to the corner and junction at the site of Camp 20. Blue sky and sun overhead, turn right and you're on the way to Carrigain's summit on the Desolation Trail. (Clouds and rain up there, turn left on Carrigain Notch Trail.) Step across the brook. This is the last water.

You begin to walk on your trip's final railroad grade. It was a short spur track from Camp 20 to a landing at the base of the mountain. The Desolation Trail leaves it and heads up steeply before the embankment that appears to have been the landing and main sled road from the area around Carrigain Pond. Thereafter, the trail follows and crosses up between connecting logging roads as you surmount the ridge.

These former roads have thick bands of trees growing along them. Seen from a distance in the East Branch valley or from heights such as Mount Bond, they look like encircling, heavier-green, contour lines in the second-growth forest.

The Desolation Trail takes you to the end of the uppermost road, where the steepest ascent begins. This angle stopped J. E. Henry's logging not because it was difficult but because it was unprofitable. Shrewd assessment of cost saved the present virgin forest bordering Desolation Trail's top ½ mile to the summit. As a climber, you may also ponder the angle, but the slow upward pace will encourage you to enjoy the trees. The summit is 2 miles from Camp 20, wooded with low spruces, and overlooked by the tower, which is no longer a glassed fire lookout but a viewing platform above the evergreens for hikers.

The views on a clear day extend for miles in all directions. You can trace the route of your previous day's hike northwest of the summit. You look across the great country preserved in the Lincoln Woods Scenic Area. More distant mountains surround it. The Franconias rise on the horizon to the west, and the Presidentials northeast. Mount Hancock is a near neighbor on the southwest, while, southward, Tripyramid and the Sandwich Range complete the circle.

Now the time has come to descend to where you started on the first day. You have 5 miles to go, and Signal Ridge will give you one more outlook.

The Signal Ridge Trail drops off the summit past the fire lookout's cabin site and well—which may have water in it, but of dubious purity. The trail continues the steep descent to Signal Ridge. There you bear left along the crest for a fine view across Carrigain Notch to the cliffs on Mount Lowell. After abrupt downward progress, the trail slabs through a logged valley, passes Carrigain Notch Trail coming in left, and goes on down to the Sawyer River Road and your parked car.

Mount Isolation

Time allowed: 3 days, 2 nights
Distance (round trip): 14 miles
Walking time: 11 hours
Vertical rise: 3,200 feet
Maps: USGS 15′ North Conway;
  USGS 15′ Crawford Notch

A high ridge to separate you from the highway, a long wooded valley with a clear stream, miles of white birches, and a remote, 4,005-foot peak south of Mount Washington—these all appear for your enjoyment on your way to the summit of Mount Isolation. You follow Rocky Branch Trail, Isolation Trail, and Davis Path on this undemanding, three-day hike. Because you return by the same route, you have the opportunity to see again the trees and brooks and views you passed hiking in; this double exposure reveals new secrets and discoveries.

First Day

NH 16 to Rocky Branch and Isolation Trail

Distance: 3½ miles
Walking time: 3 hours

Drive north 5.5 miles on NH 16 from Jackson's covered bridge toward Pinkham Notch. Past a bridge over the Ellis River and beyond a White Mountain National Forest sign, right, turn left for the Rocky Branch Trail parking up an asphalt roadway. Here you adjust your pack. It should include a tent. The Rocky Branch Shelter Number 2 is scheduled to be removed. Isolation Shelter has been taken down because it was in the Presidential Range–Dry River Wilderness.

The Rocky Branch Trail begins at the southwest corner of the parking, where a gated Forest Service road leads to the left. Fifty feet along this road, turn to your right onto the trail. It soon joins an old logging road and bears left up the slope. Look behind you and fix this corner in your mind so you won't miss it on the third day's return.

The trail takes you up west and north from the highway in a forest of beech and yellow birch. About ten minutes from your car a ski touring trail joins, left, marked with blue blazes. Again look behind you to make sure you don't take the ski touring trail when you return. It coincides with the Rocky Branch Trail for a few hundred yards, then bears right across a small stream. Keep to the left away from the logging road as your route zigzags up to another logging road, and to switchbacks often root-tangled and rocky.

Rising steadily up this unremitting series of slopes for 2 miles, the trail approaches the crossing of Rocky Branch Ridge. A left corner, westward, takes you to another ancient logging road down a slight incline, which levels across an area of springs and two streams which form Miles Brook. The trail ascends again. Spruce/fir woods begin at this elevation near the 3,000-foot sag in the main ridge, which attains 3,660 feet at an unnamed summit to the right of the trail. Across a muddy height-of-land you can avoid some of the boot-churned bog by taking an unofficial bypass left through the evergreens, and back to the trail. It dries out somewhat as you come to a sign for the wilderness area you are about to enter—The Presidential Range–Dry River Wilderness. Beyond this sign, camping must be at least 200 feet from streams, trails, and former campsites.

Descending the ridge, the trail is sometimes a running rivulet. The rounded rocks, eroded from the thin soil as far back as the days when this was first a sled road, are hazards to your footing. Occasionally, through the young trees, you can see across Rocky Branch valley to Montalban Ridge, but there's difficulty in identifying summits along it, such as Mount Davis and Mount Isolation. The trail improves greatly when it crosses a trickle of water to the left and takes to a logging road dug from the slope. This eases your way down to Rocky Branch.

There's no footbridge. You cross the stream on rocks to a ledge above pools. (This can be a dangerous crossing at high water.) Atop the bank beyond the ledge, the Isolation Trail begins on the right. (The Isolation Trail will be your upstream route on the second day.) Follow the Rocky Branch Trail sharply left along the old railroad grade for a hundred feet. The Rocky Branch Shelter Number 2 (or its site after its removal) is in a little clearing above the stream. You may seek a campsite in the vicinity, but be sure it's 200 feet from the trail, stream, clearing, and any other obviously used camping place.

Second Day

Rocky Branch to Mount Isolation

Distance: 4½ miles
Walking time: 3½ hours

Your morning hike up Rocky Branch follows the Isolation Trail from the junction just north of the site of Rocky Branch Shelter Number 2. The trail turns left up from the railroad grade until, regaining the grade, it follows that route wherever possible, but avoiding slides and washouts. A forest of white birches has taken over the blueberry barrens of fifty years ago. Under the birches, hobble bushes spread broad leaves that shade the fern fronds and the fan-like leaves of wild sarsaparilla. The valley has seen many changes: spruce logging, then the fires of 1914 and the scorched earth they brought, blueberry bushes, sprouting poplar and wild cherry growth, and now tall white birches where the old spruces grew.

The Isolation Trail goes up the valley of Rocky Branch for about 1½ miles. (In less than this distance, however, the Forest Service is considering a new route more directly west toward Mount Isolation and to the Davis Path near it.) The former logging railroad and trail cross Rocky Branch several times. The log trestles are gone, and now you step from rock to rock, or wade. Occasional sections of the trail keep to the side of the hill on the east bank for rough but somewhat dryer footing above the stream. Large boulders here and there interrupt the flowing water and form pools below alder thickets. You walk in a long grove of white birches.

Beyond the final crossing to the west bank, the trail leads into spruces and over damp ground along a tributary brook. As the flow of water dwindles you should consider selecting a place for

View from Mt. Isolation

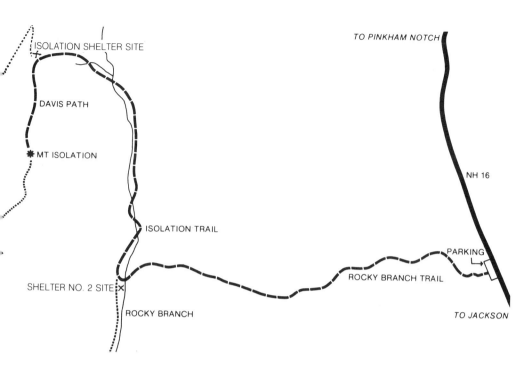

your tent. Although the tributary stream you're following can be said to have its source near the site of the former Isolation Shelter, this spring, which supplied hikers, has sometimes been dry. I suggest you set up your tent—of course 200 feet away from the trail and stream and in a spot never used by other hikers. Then continue up the Isolation Trail to the site of the shelter and the Davis Path. At the junction you reach an elevation of 3,757 feet. Clear skies here on this second day of your trip mean that you eat a quick lunch and head for Mount Isolation. If rain is falling you'll want to postpone the climb until morning. Mount Isolation is only ¾ mile south on the Davis Path. This trail runs left and right (south and north) through the site's clearing. Turn left onto the Davis Path. (The Isolation Trail at the site turns north,

right, and for a quarter-mile coincides with the Davis Path before it forks left, west, and descends to the Dry River Trail. The Davis Path extends from US 302 in Crawford Notch to Mount Washington. For the section just north of US 302 see Hike 45, Mount Crawford.)

Stay on the Davis Path. It climbs a spruce ridge overlooking Rocky Branch valley, left. But keep your eye on the trail. Watch for a spur trail right, at a small cairn. It takes you scrambling up through spruce scrub to the flat rocky summit of Mount Isolation.

The spruce scrub offers no obstacle to the outlook as you step across the ledges. The western horizon at once draws and holds your attention. The southern peaks of the Presidential Range begin in the south near Crawford Notch at Mount Jackson and extend north to

Clinton, Eisenhower, Franklin, and Monroe, in a long serrated array to the great peak of Washington, which strikes into the sky four miles north of you. Mount Isolation places you high between two valleys that sweep down from Mount Washington to Crawford Notch; the line of summits, near whose northern end you stand, is named Montalban Ridge. You have hiked the valley to the east, Rocky Branch; to the west between you and the southern peaks, you look into Dry River valley, which isn't dry. Its upper waters are apparent as cascades on the headwall of Oakes Gulf between you and Mounts Monroe and Washington. (Dry River can quickly become a raging torrent. It bears another, more appropriate name: Mount Washington River.)

Mount Isolation is a grandstand seat for cloud shows. Often, white wisps and tumbling fogs swirl among the southern peaks. On some bright, clear days, storm clouds suddenly mass around Washington's cone and obscure the buildings and towers. If the storm threatens rain on Mount Isolation, retreat to your tent. Retrace your way east down the spur trail and turn left onto the Davis Path. The site of the former shelter is twenty minutes away. Turn right onto the Isolation Trail for the protection of the tent you've pitched away from the tributary to the Rocky Branch.

Third Day

Davis Path–Isolation Trail Junction to NH 16

Distance: 6 miles
Walking time: 4½ hours

Perhaps this morning brings clear skies after a previous rainy afternoon that kept you from Mount Isolation. You still have time to go up it, because this third day's hike is almost as moderate as the previous days'.

If you're early enough to Mount Isolation, you'll see the sunrise brightening Mount Washington, or maybe a shining white cloud around the peak. If rain pours down this morning, and you really want to reach the summit, you'll just have to slog along through the downpour. You'd be wiser to wait for another chance. There's nothing to see on Mount Isolation in a rainstorm except spruce scrub, ledges, Labrador tea, and mountain cranberry.

For the return hike, walk back down the Isolation Trail to Rocky Branch, and down the stream to the junction with the Rocky Branch Trail. Turn left onto the Rocky Branch Trail, cross the stream, and climb over the ridge. Then it's all downhill to NH 16 and your car—but avoid the ski touring trail, and turn right off the logging road just above the parking area.

50

The Mahoosuc Range

Time allowed: 7 days, 6 nights
Distance: 33 miles
Walking time: 32 hours
Vertical rise: 8,600 feet*
Maps: USGS 7½' Berlin; USGS 7½' Shelburne; USGS
   7½' Gilead (Me.); USGS 15' Old Speck Mtn. (Me.)

For many years the Mahoosuc Range was little known except to the "through-hikers" of the Appalachian Trail, who said it was the toughest thirty miles between Maine and Georgia. Never a part of the White Mountain National Forest, this range is now federally protected as a segment of the Appalachian National Scenic Trail.

The town of Gorham and the Androscoggin River separate Mount Madison and Mount Moriah from the westernmost of the Mahoosucs, Mount Hayes. The AT, descending from Mount Moriah south of the Androscoggin, crosses at Shelburne east of Gorham on US 2. The AT follows the Centennial Trail toward Mount Hayes for the first 3¾ miles of this 33-mile backpack over the summits of the range to Grafton Notch and ME 26 north of Newry, Maine. From Mount Hayes the AT follows the AMC's Mahoosuc Trail.

The distance as the crow flies is only 18 miles. Allowing for the walking distances to ascend and descend at the ends of the range, and a southerly swing

and some zigzags from peak to peak, the extra, remaining 11 miles are up and down along the range.

The varied worlds along the way include hardwood forests, mountain meadows, spruce-shaded slopes, subarctic barrens, frequent ledges, sharp ravines, and summit after summit. The Mahoosucs are a unique experience. Leisurely travel enhances the experience; the Mahoosucs deserve a week. Of the seven days allotted, you hike six days with time to relax at intervals and still make camp long before dark. One day is a spare. Use it when a storm engulfs the range by taking refuge in a tent or in one of the four shelters. If your week's weather turns out to be perfect, you have a day to rest and loaf at Speck Pond's shelter before completing the Mahoosuc Range on Old Speck Mountain and descending to Grafton Notch, where you meet asphalt again on ME 26.

Transportation arrangements will vary to fit individual plans. You can leave your car parked near the trail at Grafton Notch and be driven around west to Shelburne. You may plan to be met at Grafton Notch on the seventh day.

Although either Shelburne or Grafton Notch could be the starting point, the

* This is an estimate based on map contour counting; the rises are frequent.

northeast direction from Mount Hayes has one specific advantage. Progress northeastward gives you an exciting sense of increasing wildness. With this you also enjoy a continual, although intermittent, ascent: Mount Hayes, 2,566 feet; Mount Success, 3,590 feet; Old Speck, 4,180 feet; with ten other summits in between.

The Mahoosuc Range has become a "laboratory" for AMC research on trail use and methods for preserving the mountain environment. First with the cooperation of the Brown Company, and more recently with the James River Company, AMC has replaced old shelters, built tent platforms, and improved the trail with stone steps and stairs and log walkways as well as with waterbars for erosion control, in keeping with AT standards as the Appalachian National Scenic Trail. (There is now a small fee for overnight stays at Speck Pond Campsite, and until recently also at Gentian Pond Shelter and tent sites.) They have also installed boxes with cards at the trails' starts to check the number of hikers using them. It's a good program and needs your assistance—the cards take just a few minutes to fill out. Of course, carry out your trash, keep campsites clean, and help the caretaker when there is one.

The plan of this backpack takes you to shelters for five of the six nights. You will need your tent, however, at Trident Col Tent Site, and probably near the shelters if they are fully occupied when you arrive. Also, you may require the tent for protection in an emergency such as an injury or a severe storm. Otherwise, no camping is allowed except at authorized locations. Fires are allowed only at shelters and at Trident Col Tent Site. Backpacker stoves may be used along the trail for a hot meal, and are almost a necessity at the shelters if the fireplace is in use when you want to cook.

Concerning your outfit, I will point out

that it should be as light as possible, consistent with carrying plenty of food, water, and adequate equipment. Your tent, stove, cooking utensils, sleeping bag, rain gear, clothing, and the backpack itself *must* be tested and reliable. None of them can be replaced. If you are not an experienced backpacker, I suggest that you try out both equipment and similar food on at least two shakedown trips before going on this one. Two other admonishments occur to me. One necessity always in short supply along the summits of the Mahoosucs is water. Sources are few, far between, and except at shelters, often unreliable. You'll need more water bottles than for ordinary hikes. Next, fitness. Obviously, strength and endurance for heavy backpacking are absolutely necessary to insure both safety and enjoyment.

These comments about the demand that the Mahoosucs make on you and your outfit are meant not to discourage you but to advise on the measures you should take for a happy and rewarding backpack.

First Day

Hogan Road, Shelburne, to Mount Hayes, Cascade Mountain, and Trident Col Tent Site

Distance: 8 miles
Walking time: 6 hours

You'll want to be at this Shelburne trailhead early in the morning, perhaps from overnight accommodations nearby. The day's backpack will be long but not overly strenuous or rugged.

Drive US 2 to North Road in Shelburne. North Road's western junction with US 2 is 3.5 miles east of Gorham. (Parking for the Rattle River Trail, the route of the AT south, is about 300 yards farther east on US 2.) Turn north onto North Road and drive across the bridge over the Androscoggin River. At .5 mile from US 2, turn left onto Hogan Road. Drive this rough dirt road for ¼ mile to parking spaces, mostly on the left. The Centennial Trail begins on the north side of the road as a wide pathway remaining from former logging operations.

This is the last chance to check your equipment and food and water. Take an ample day's requirement of water. There may be none on the trail until Trident Col Tent Site.

The Centennial Trail was named for the AMC's hundredth anniversary, when it was laid out and cut in 1976. After 150 feet along the pathway, turn left at a sign where the woods road continues straight ahead. You are on a trail now. It winds up through a hardwood forest. The white AT blazes lead you upward over stone steps past ledges on the right to the first lookoff on the left, across the lake formed by a dam in the Androscoggin bisected by the Canadian National Railroad—the former Grand Trunk. Face around and follow a short section of trail north to an old logging road, which the Centennial follows to the left. Views and occasional steps alternate with easy slabbing of the contours as you walk through beech woods. Some of the gray, smooth trunks show old marks of claws dug in by bears climbing eagerly for beechnuts. On several ledges you'll walk over the brass plugs that identify the Appalachian National Scenic Trail.

At last above a jumble of rock slabs you get the first glimpses of the Mahoosucs rising away ahead of you to the east. The trail curves up into open spaces among scrubby spruces to a bare knob, then on through birches to the junction among sparse evergreens at the Mahoosuc Trail from Mount Hayes and Gorham.

Here you may leave your pack and follow the Mahoosuc Trail west over the summit of Hayes to the cliffs above

Gorham and the wide easterly bend of the Androscoggin south of the smoking papermills of Berlin. Away west, Madison, Adams, and Washington rise magnificently stark and barren at the summits. You look south to Pinkham Notch and the Carter-Moriah Range forming the notch's eastern slope. This side jaunt over Hayes will take about forty-five minutes, but worth it on a clear day, and I've included the distance and time in the total.

Back at the junction with the Centennial Trail, shoulder your pack and head north on the Mahoosuc Trail, which is now the AT. It descends from the bare ledges, blueberry bushes, and evergreens of Mount Hayes into the leafy woods of the col between Hayes and Cascade Mountain. This col might better be described with the woodsman's term "sag" rather than the mountaineer's "col." It's a low wooded valley between the two mountains. Water may trickle below the lowest point of the sag into pools (if any) deep enough to give you water by the cupful.

Next comes Cascade Mountain. The beeches and yellow and white birches change to small, park-like maples, then to bushes and broken slabs of rock. From here you'll be treated to a special sunset show. The Androscoggin valley begins to close in with shadows. You stand far above, and look across to the Presidentials sharply etched by western sunlight. Move on along the ridge through spruce woods alternating with ledges and damp sphagnum moss. At the east shoulder, the Mahoosuc Trail drops steeply toward a view of distant peaks and ridges. The descent pushes your pack against your shoulders, and your hands seek steadying holds on bushes and trees, until the trail levels out at Trident Col. A spur trail leads left to water and four tent sites. This will be your camping place.

Second Day

Trident Col Tent Site to Gentian Pond Shelter.

Distance: 5 miles
Walking time: 4 hours

The Mahoosuc Trail the next morning leads on eastward by an old logging road, descending somewhat and slabbing south of middle Trident Peak. You cross trickles of water here and there through the hardwoods. The trail takes you up to a more recent, bulldozed road, which, after a short distance, bears right. The trail branches left, and you follow it among bushes and young trees up a gradual slope to a level section. The approach to Page Pond through tall grass shows you first the spruce ridge beyond, then the oval of water. In late summertime, closed gentians bloom near the beaver dam. Depending on the latest beaver work, the trail may cross over the dam's poles and mud.

An easy walk among spruces brings you to the base of the next height, Wocket Ledge, where the ridge rears up suddenly. You dig for footholds and test spruce roots and branches for secure hand grips. The ledge itself appears at the crest 50 yards to the left, about ¾ mile from Page Pond. The climb has been strenuous, and you'll want to sit for

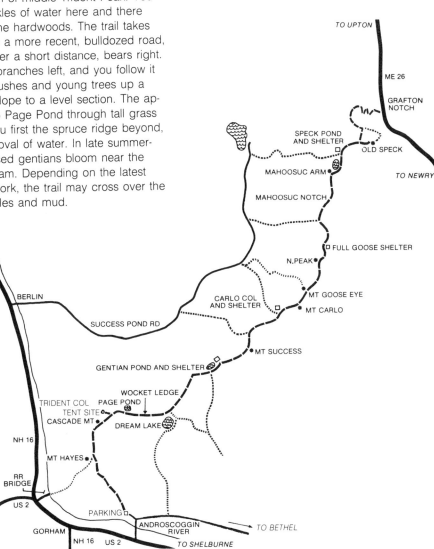

Panorama of the Mahoosuc Range

a while and look off at the wild country near and far.

Back to the trail and up beyond the open ledge, you follow the trail in spruces. Descending, you pass a spring and the beginning of a Peabody Brook branch. Ascending and descending—the theme of the Mahoosucs—you slant down to a mountain pond called Dream Lake.

The trail turns left along the lake shore. By stepping quietly through bushes down to the water, perhaps you see a moose feeding, belly-deep in the lake. If only lily pads and quiet ripples meet your eyes, proceed along the trail and across the inlet to the northeast end. There the Peabody Brook Trail terminates at the Mahoosuc Trail. (The Peabody Brook Trail comes up from North Road in Shelburne off US 2.) A short walk down Peabody Brook Trail takes you to a striking camera shot across Dream Lake to Mount Washington.

Returning to the Mahoosuc Trail, you head east along the inlet brook. The trail is damp, but log walkways offer dry footing. It swings left across a bog, again on walkways above the water, to a low ridge. The trail's up-and-down windings take you to a height of land so flat and swampy as to be almost imperceptible. The new watershed's first display appears at the boggy inlet to Moss Pond, formerly Upper Gentian Pond. You leave the shoreline for a rough, northern traverse back in the evergreens till you return to the pond near the outlet. There on your right you see a beaver dam so high that it seems barely to hold the brimming little basin from pouring down the mountainside. The dam has been doing this for many years. Two beaver lodges on the far shore house the caretakers.

The trail follows the outlet brook a short distance. Then as your way turns left, your attention will be occupied by the massive boulders it meanders among

during the steep descent. A turn to the right leads you away from a cliff among white and yellow birches and swamp maples to Gentian Pond. You approach massive ledges and a gap in the rock, which carries away the outlet water. A little log bridge crosses where once beavers built a dam. You can see Gentian Pond Shelter on its rocky perch above you.

The shelter and its outside fireplace of piled stones rest on an abrupt, wooded dropoff, which falls away so steeply that you have a splendid view to the Androscoggin River far below in its wide valley. (From Gentian Pond Shelter, the Austin Brook Trail descends to Shelburne's North Road. Your northeast backpack in the morning will take you beyond this last trail south from the Mahoosucs.)

The pond water is handy and serves well enough to rinse yourself. For drinking water you follow a faint path a good distance north among the shore spruces to an inlet trickling clear and cold past green sphagnum moss.

Third Day

Gentian Pond Shelter to Carlo Col Shelter

Distance: 5¾ miles
Walking time: 6½ hours

Mount Success is your big objective after breakfast at Gentian Pond Shelter. The climb measures the mountain's bulk rather than its height, which is a moderate 3,590 feet. The up-and-down approach makes you think that the mountain has retreated beyond ridges to fortify itself against your attack.

In early morning, a steep climb places you on ledges above the pond. Then you descend and climb again over the first of two rugged little hills protruding from the mountainside. After the second knob, a little rivulet provides a canteen filling: no more certain water until the end of the day's hike at Carlo Col Shelter.

The trail continues, steep and difficult. You surmount blocks of granite, which obstruct the way and indicate an old slide. Then you cross a washout grown to brush, and begin to climb in the spruce/fir forest. The damp woods are the habitat of the deliberate spruce grouse. The trees dwindle to evergreen scrub at open ledges, and you climb toward the summit through more scrub and over bare rock.

Mount Success spreads before you northern vistas of lakes and wilderness as well as an unusual perspective toward the Presidentials. The summit itself presents the first muddy areas typical of high Mahoosuc ridges above tree line. Lying in hollows between rock faces, the black earth has a dry crust in hot weather. Stay on the split-log walkways or you'll be into ankle-deep muck. Various heath plants border this rich humus. Matted dwarf spruces testify to the severe winds.

From Mount Success, the Mahoosuc Trail turns left down a barren shoulder into scrub and taller evergreens. The trail is rocky and at times closed in by luxuriant spruce/fir branches. Several boggy areas can be extremely wet after rain. You level out and descend into a col and junction with the Success Trail on your left. (The Success Trail is the first of five trails from the Mahoosuc Trail to the Success Pond Road, here three miles north. This paper company road runs northeast fourteen miles from Berlin to the pond.)

For the next 1¼ miles, the Mahoosuc Trail follows a northeast ridge. You climb and slab wooded contours, then descend, only to climb and descend again. In a little hollow an AT sign marks the New Hampshire–Maine line. After some rugged climbing, the trail takes you to a north outlook on bare rock surrounded by scrub and Labrador tea bushes. The view is across the vast north country.

Now the final climb down this ledge to Carlo Col gives any backpacker cause for thought. You may wisely decide to take off your pack and lower it to a companion who has made his way down, packless, by clinging to spruces and gripping with both hands on finger-holds of rock while groping for footholds below. A few yards farther on, after you have reorganized yourself, you step into the deep cleft of Carlo Col. You are near your night's shelter. Turn left onto the Carlo Col Trail and follow it down a stony ¼ mile. At the first sure water the trail bears left to avoid it because it has taken over the old trail. From a little ridge you descend in a wide curve to the right and return to the streamlet. Continue straight across and up a steep bank to Carlo Col Shelter. (The Carlo Col Trail descends on the left beside the water to Success Pond Road 2½ miles away.) The Carlo Col Shelter is built of logs like Gentian Pond Shelter.

Fourth Day

Carlo Col Shelter to Full Goose Shelter

Distance: 4½ miles
Walking time: 4 hours

This day's hike features Mount Goose Eye and barren ridges such as you might see in Labrador. It begins with a starting climb from Carlo Col Shelter back to the Mahoosuc Trail. You'll feel the morning coolness because the shelter is 3,000 feet high. Turn left from the Carlo Col Trail onto the Mahoosuc Trail. Mount Carlo, elevation 3,562, rises ahead, and the trail leads up through spruces. But the climb warms you before you emerge on Mount Carlo's bare summit, perhaps hidden in morning mist. You've been climbing forty-five minutes if you start your day sensibly, without straining, so clearing skies and valleys may reveal the northern panorama of Success Pond and the mountains you saw yesterday afternoon before Carlo Col.

Beyond the summit, the trail crosses a bog on split log walkways, descending into spruce woods, then up a ledge and down again, often through more black mud or above it on walkways. You come out onto a barren slope, which if horizontal and near the Arctic Circle could be called tundra. Your eyes are at once attracted to Mount Goose Eye ahead across a deep col—a distant pinnacle of rock.

Legend gives this mountain the early name of "Goose High," because the summit was an obstacle to migrating geese. If so, the geese had to clear by a few wingbeats a rocky 3,860-foot mass.

The descent from the barrens into evergreens becomes so steep and rough that you grab at spruces to help you swing down. Don't forget to test before entrusting serious weight and balance to a tree. As you approach the transition to the col, you may find water trickling across the trail from a spring on the left. The walk across the col beside wide patches of sphagnum moss near the spruces will take you only five minutes. Then Mount Goose Eye!

You can test your leg muscles on the stone steps, which offer steady climbing. The steepness eases at a swing left, then up you go again. Mount Goose Eye shows you how to climb (with the aid of AT trail crew work) 500 feet in ¼ mile.

There are more walkways, leading to more stone steps, which bear right to avoid a chimney in the mountainside. At the upper end of the stone steps, carefully climb to the log stairs. You emerge on a less demanding section, which takes you to open views over low scrub and ledges. Ahead, Goose Eye's pinnacle appears clearly. There's a last scramble in the scrub and you top out

on the east shoulder of the mountain at treeline.

The Mahoosuc Trail turns sharp right. Branching left, the Goose Eye Trail leads over the summit rocks. (And down to the Success Pond Road.) You'll want to dump your pack at the junction and climb the 200 yards to Goose Eye's peak for a rest, a snack, and the views.

Return to your pack and continue east on the Mahoosuc Trail. You walk along a rocky ridge, bare except for scattered small spruces, and you can see your next climb—East Peak. But first you traverse a section of evergreens to a col, then ascend to the bare summit. On it there's a left turn, north, down from East Peak. Watch for cairns. The trail descends across a great sloping barrens, toward the eastern corner of spruces. The seemingly subarctic flora and shrubs along the trail are so low you look off to your next destination, North Peak, and in the distance to northern forests and lakes.

You enter the scrub you've been approaching. The trail drops to the col before North Peak. The woods open up among larger spruces. At a damp wooded ravine, you come upon small pools of water cupped in sphagnum moss. If the moss has absorbed all the water, a handful squeezed above a cup produces a drink.

North Peak is steep, too. The wide barrens resemble treeline areas in the Presidentials and Franconias, although here vegetation extends to the highest ground. Much of the rock is crumbly and soft. Gravel in the trail crunches under your boots.

Clouds and rain often settle over the range, and winds are icy. If you must brave a drenching exposure on a ridge such as Goose Eye's North Peak, you face subarctic winds and temperatures.

From North Peak, the Mahoosuc Trail continues east along open ground beyond the summit. You follow and descend through scrub and barrens into head-high spruces. You find yourself walking down over ledges among older trees. Another mountain looms before you. The trail seems to vanish, however, at a wall of brush, and you are hemmed in by a small ledge on your right.

Face the ledge and pull yourself up. You emerge by Full Goose Shelter where you'll spend the night. It opens toward Fulling Mill Mountain and the precipitous valleys of Bull Branch and Goose Eye Brook. Beyond are the mountains that rise above and conceal Grafton Notch.

This shelter for ten hikers is built of boards and sawn timbers. To get a drink of water walk past the front and take the steep path down to the spring.

Fifth Day

Full Goose Shelter to Speck Pond Shelter

Distance: 5 miles
Walking time: 7 hours

The Mahoosuc Trail continues north from Full Goose Shelter by dropping down the overlook in front of the shelter, to a ravine that is only an infinitesimal hint of the Mahoosuc Notch to come. But first, Fulling Mill Mountain. You climb up a steady grade through evergreens and reach a meadow between two wooded summits. The trail turns left and you rapidly descend, in trees again, 1,000 feet to the western end of Mahoosuc Notch. (At a junction, left, the Notch Trail comes in from the Success Pond Road.)

You turn sharply right and follow the Mahoosuc Trail down a pleasant slope among spruces at 2,500 feet elevation. You are entering Mahoosuc Notch. The gentle approach leaves you unprepared for the gigantic rock slabs and chunks, which seem to have fallen from the high cliffs on either side. But they have not fallen recently; they are draped with

moss and crusted with lichens.

The moss forms treacherous pads over crevices and caves. Be careful not to step on any moss that reaches from slab to slab. As you crawl under overhanging rocks, you hear water trickling deep down in caves. Winter chill comes to you from the ice caverns. You follow white paint marks as the trail twists and turns for 1 mile among the rocks. You should plan on at least two hours during which you'll be busy reaching for handholds, stepping wide, balancing, and creeping.

At the Notch's eastern end, you resume normal woods hiking. The trail follows the brook past the site of a former small beaver pond. Below this, after entering big hardwoods, you turn left away from the brook, climb up a short distance, and bear right onto an old logging road. In a slabbing ascent, the trail rounds Mahoosuc Mountain.

The trail follows a logging road toward a sag known as Notch 2, until you cross a brook. After a rough section, you begin the day's second real climb as the trail swings up Mahoosuc Arm. Much of the way, the trail rises among tall, old spruces. Mahoosuc Arm extends 1,200 feet above Mahoosuc Notch. About halfway, or ¾ mile from the Notch, you come to a seasonal brook in a rock sluice; don't count on water.

Climbing on, you enter evergreen scrub and begin to ascend sloping ledges. The trail follows cairns along rock worn by glaciers and ages of weathering. You come out on the bare ridge itself, Mahoosuc Arm, which is really a mountain almost 3,800 feet high.

A big cairn and post on the open ledges mark the summit of Mahoosuc Arm. Here the Mahoosuc Trail turns right. (A cutoff trail to Speck Pond Trail forks left.) The Mahoosuc Trail jogs approximately south and then north along the ridge and enters occasional scrub between open meadows. Now going down more steeply through spruce woods, you descend to 3,500 feet and Speck Pond. The trail circles to the east shore, and at the upper end you come to Speck Pond Campsite, which includes the shelter for twelve hikers, tent sites, and caretaker. There is a small fee for overnight camping. A small, deep, mountain lake, Speck Pond is the highest in Maine, and has been measured fifty feet to the bottom. Beavers may raise the depth at times with a dam in the outlet, which is Bull Branch. The pond reflects the surrounding pointed spruces, or sometimes, due to its elevation, lies smothered in clouds. (The Speck Pond Trail leaves from the shelter for the Success Pond Road.)

Sixth Day

Allowed for bad weather or to spend at Speck Pond

Seventh Day

Speck Pond Shelter to Grafton Notch

Distance: 4¾ miles
Walking time: 4½ hours

Your departure in the morning should be adjusted to the weather. Foggy daylight and gloomy spruce woods have been known to brighten in an hour, and too-eager hikers have arrived at Old Speck's summit to find it shrouded in clouds, and by then descending to Grafton Notch have missed the spectacular scenery spread out in all directions from the observation tower. Now that you have been conditioned by the Mahoosucs, you should be able to climb Old Speck and descend to Grafton Notch in four and one-half hours. So wait awhile for clear skies.

Take the Mahoosuc Trail from Speck Pond Campsite northeast. Directly, it climbs a large knoll, drops down, and then up and around another ridge. In the next little valley, you pass a spring east of the trail. You begin to climb up Old Speck along ledges that lead you on upward at the apex of their angles, which drop off on either side.

This rocky shoulder joins spruce woods, and the trail, bearing right, leads into them. The trail parallels for a time the blue paint blazes identifying the boundary of Grafton Notch State Park. You are nearing the highest elevation of your backpack week—4,180 feet. As you approach the summit of Old Speck, you pass on your left the Old Speck Trail to Grafton Notch and the highway, ME 26. This trail will be the route of your descent. From this junction to the summit, a little over ¼ mile, you may as well carry your pack along the more level section to the clearing in the evergreens surrounding the observation tower.

The view northward from the tower is toward Lake Umbagog and the Rangeley Lakes, whose waters shine like mirrors on a sunny day. To the southwest, the peaks, ravines, and barren heaths of the rugged range you've climbed over stretch away to the Presidentials.

From the summit clearing, retrace your steps along the Mahoosuc Trail to the Old Speck Trail. Turn right onto the Old Speck Trail for your 3½-mile downward loop to the depths of Grafton Notch. First the trail takes you steeply down to a long northern ridge. As you begin this, the trail turns northwest where the Link Trail enters on your right. (The Link Trail gives steep access to the site of the former cabin for the fire warden near a small brook, about ¼ mile. At the site, a trail from the summit's East Spur joins with the Link Trail.)

Walk past the Link Trail along the northern ridge for about ½ mile, with steady, sometimes rough, loss of altitude in the spruce/fir forest. The trail swings eastward among tall spruces and leaves the ridge at an outlook into the notch and down the Bear River valley to Newry, and nearby across the notch, to Baldpate Mountain. The Eyebrow Trail comes in on your left. (The Eyebrow Trail traverses the upper edge of an 800-foot cliff called The Eyebrow, and is not for backpackers.) Climb down to the right of the Eyebrow Trail junction on the Old Speck Trail. Stone steps and water bars and log steps will assist you for the remaining mile of this section, which has almost literally been attached to the mountainside by trail crews.

You cross a small stream, the head of Cascade Brook. The trail turns left and follows the south edge of the rock that carries the cascades. Then a right turn puts you on more log steps leading down into yellow birches and beeches. These deciduous trees indicate you've come down to a milder climate. The trail follows a series of switchbacks.

Grafton Notch is so narrow that you have scarcely a hundred yards—after you pass the lower Eyebrow Trail entering on your left—of level walking till you reach the bulletin board and outline trail map, and step out onto the large parking area for the Grafton Notch State Park. (From the bulletin board, the AT continues east across ME 26 to climb over Baldpate Mountain on its way to Katahdin.)

Now you are back in the world of wheeled transportation for the first time in a week.

Guidebooks from Backcountry Publications

Written for people of all ages and experience, these popular and carefully prepared book feature detailed trail and tour directions, notes on points of interest and natural phenomena maps and photographs.

Walks and Rambles Series

Walks and Rambles on The Delmarva Peninsula, by Jay Abercrombie $8.95

Walks and Rambles in Westchester (NY) and Fairfield (CT) Counties, by Kaye Anderson $7.95

Walks and Rambles in Rhode Island, by Ken Weber $8.95

25 Walks in the Dartmouth-Lake Sunapee Region, by Mary L. Kibling $4.95

Biking Series

25 Bicycle Tours in Maine, by Howard Stone $8.95

25 Bicycle Tours in Vermont, by John Freidin $7.95

25 Bicycle Tours in New Hampshire, by Tom and Susan Heavey $6.95

25 Bicycle Tours in the Finger Lakes, by Mark Roth and Sally Waters $6.95

25 Bicycle Tours in and around New York City, by Dan Carlinsky and David Heim $6.95

25 Bicycle Tours in Eastern Pennsylvania, by Dale Adams and Dale Speicher $6.95

Canoeing Series

Canoe Camping Vermont and New Hampshire Rivers, by Roioli Schweiker $6.95

Canoeing Central New York, by William P. Ehling $8.95

Canoeing Massachusetts, Rhode Island and Connecticut, by Ken Weber $7.95

Hiking Series

Discover the South Central Adirondacks, by Barbara McMartin $8.95

Discover the Adirondacks 2, by Barbara McMartin $7.95

50 Hikes in the Adirondacks, by Barbara McMartin $9.95

50 Hikes in Central New York, by William P. Ehling $8.95

50 Hikes in the Hudson Valley, by Barbara McMartin and Peter Kick $9.95

50 Hikes in Central Pennsylvania, by Tom Thwaites $9.95

50 Hikes in Eastern Pennsylvania, by Carolyn Hoffman $8.95

50 Hikes in Western Pennsylvania, by Tom Thwaites $8.95

50 Hikes in Maine, by John Gibson $8.95

50 Hikes in the White Mountains, by Daniel Doan $9.95

50 More Hikes in New Hampshire, by Daniel Doan $9.95

50 Hikes in Vermont, 3rd edition, revised by the Green Mountain Club $8.95

50 Hikes in Massachusetts, by John Brady and Brian White $9.95

50 Hikes in Connecticut, by Gerry and Sue Hardy $8.95

50 Hikes in West Virginia, by Ann and Jim McGraw $9.95

The above titles are available at bookstores and at certain sporting goods stores or may be ordered directly from the publisher. For complete descriptions of these and other guides, write: Backcountry Publications, P.O. Box 175, Woodstock, VT 05091.